S T U D E N T - F R I E N D L Y

Write Great Essays!

Write Great Essays!

Second Edition

Peter Levin

Open University Press

Open University Press
McGraw-Hill Education
McGraw-Hill House
Shoppenhangers Road
Maidenhead
Berkshire
England
SL6 2QL

email: enquiries@openup.co.uk
world wide web: www.openup.co.uk

and Two Penn Plaza, New York, NY 10121–2289, USA

First edition published 2004
Copyright © Peter Levin 2009

A catalogue record of this book is available from the British Library

ISBN–13: 978-0-335-23727-2 (pb)
ISBN–10: 033523727-4 (pb)

Library of Congress Cataloging-in-Publication Data
CIP data applied for

Fictitious names of companies, products, people, characters and/or data that may be used herein (in case studies or in examples) are not intended to represent any real individual, company, product or event.

Typeset by YHT Ltd, London
Printed in the UK by Bell and Bain Ltd, Glasgow

Mixed Sources
Product group from well-managed
forests and other controlled sources
www.fsc.org Cert no. TT-COC-002769
© 1996 Forest Stewardship Council

FSC

The *McGraw-Hill* Companies

Contents

Contents

Tables

Boxes

The strange world of the university — Read this first!

The world of the university – the 'academic world' – is a world of its own. It's very different from the 'real world' in which you and I and most other people exist. If you're a student, it's crucial to your success that you are aware of the many differences between the two worlds and can move easily between them.

'Out there, in the real world, things happen and things change.' In the real world, people live and work, raise children, play or watch sport, go clubbing, and so on. There are lots of other human activities and processes going on as well, like manufacturing and trading and communicating and providing services of many kinds. Out there too are a host of natural phenomena: to do with the weather, all kinds of matter and energy, chemical reactions, the birth, growth and death of living things – you name it!

The academic world, on the other hand, is full of 'mental constructs': descriptions, theories and explanations, ideas and critiques. You and I can't experience such mental constructs in the same way as we experience the real world, directly, through seeing, hearing, touching, tasting, smelling. Instead we have to get them into our heads through the medium of – in particular – the written word and the spoken word, via books and articles and web pages, and the lectures that academics give. 'It is a peculiarity of academic learning that its focus is not the real world itself but others' views of that world.'[1]

What this means is that in the academic world you'll be learning at second hand, so to speak, rather than through your own experience, as you do in the real world. Learning at second hand does not come naturally to most people. You need some help. Sadly, such help is in short supply in the academic world. The series of Student-Friendly Guides, of which this book was the first, is designed to fill that gap.

But differences in ways of learning are far from being the only differences between the academic world and the real world. You think you can read, right? In the academic world, you're probably wrong, on two counts.

First, if you're at university in an English-speaking country you may have the impression that the books and articles you're told or recommended to read are in English. Certainly the words and grammar look like English, but don't be misled: they're actually written in 'academic-speak'. Academic-speak is a long way removed from day-to-day spoken and written English. In particular, it makes far more use of abstract words and expressions: they exist in people's minds but don't have a physical or concrete existence. So reading academic-speak is not the same as reading ordinary English. You've got to translate as you read, so it's much more like reading a foreign language, with lots of looking up words in the dictionary and puzzling over the grammar. It's a slow process at first, inevitably. It takes time to become fluent.

What makes matters worse is that every subject has its own particular academic-speak. So if you're taking courses in several subjects, you have several 'foreign languages' to get used to. Don't let this discourage you: most people manage it! The secret is to be aware of what's going on: it makes those times when you feel you're not making progress much easier to cope with.

Second, you may arrive at university taking it for granted that 'reading' means something like 'starting a book at page 1 and reading all the way through to the end'. Beware! 'Reading' in the academic world means using books to find what you want in them. If you try to read everything on your 'reading lists' all the way through then you're heading for a nervous breakdown. Think of reading as a treasure hunt: an active search for what you want rather than an attempt to soak up and absorb everything you come across.

Other words, too, have strange meanings in the academic world. You think 'discuss' and 'argue' refer to conversations with other people? Forget it! In most essay-requiring subjects you'll have to discuss and produce arguments on your own.

In the academic world, students come and – after a time, when they've completed their courses – go. The academics (faculty, teaching staff) mostly stick around for much longer. You may feel, having met a few, that academics are, by and large, a somewhat strange bunch. I have to say that that's my feeling too. They're certainly very individual (have you heard the joke that organizing academics is like herding cats?) many to the point of being idiosyncratic if not actually eccentric. Almost all of them are people who themselves did well as students at university and are now doing research as well as teaching. So the chances are that they're (a) quite talented at their subjects, and (b) quite preoccupied with their research work, especially as almost all academics get promotion on the basis of their research publications, not their teaching achievements.[2]

This can create quite a few problems for students. The pressure on academics to produce publications and perform administrative duties limits the time and energy they can put into teaching. Moreover, talented people, people who have an intuitive flair for their subject, can be really poor at explaining it, because when they were students themselves, they were able to tackle it by leaps and bounds: they didn't have to go slowly, step by step, as mere mortals do. Although many academics are dedicated to teaching, most of them have had little or no training in how to teach. And what training there is conspicuously omits what is arguably the most important skill of all for a teacher, that of empathizing and developing rapport, without which a teacher has no chance of being able to put himself or herself in the shoes (and head) of a student grappling with a task.

As a student, you may also find that academics distance themselves from you in all sorts of ways. Unless you're really fortunate, you'll be treated not as a junior member of a learning community but as if you belong to a separate species. You'll be a distraction from research, a burden ('workload'). You'll be treated as one of the masses, to whom education is to be 'delivered'. You'll be someone in an audience, listening or trying to take notes while the speaker engages in that one-way mode of communication beloved of academics, telling other people what's what. You may well find, like many students, that the feedback you get on your work isn't satisfactory.[3] In all probability it'll be mostly criticism rather than appreciation, focusing on bad points and ignoring the good ones, while at the same time not helping you to see what to do if you're to get better marks for your next piece of work. And at exam time you may experience the relationship with your teachers as a kind of game, in which you have to work out for yourself what the rules are for winning: what the examiners' expectations are, what approach, style, etc. will be rewarded and what will be penalized.

I suspect that all institutions are capable of messing up the lives of the people who work for and within them. I don't see universities as an exception to this rule. At some point, different academics will be giving you different and conflicting advice about some aspect of your work. And there will be mixed messages to look out for. For example, you may be given group projects to work on to develop your 'teamwork skills', and at the same time be warned very strictly against collaborating with other students on writing tasks: this is regarded as 'collusion' and will be punished!

Does all this sound very gloomy? I can't pretend that I don't think that the culture of higher education in the UK is in serious need of reform: I do. But for you that's a side issue. If you're to succeed as a student the first thing you have to do is to appreciate the nature of the system you've signed up to, which is why I felt it important to be absolutely realistic about it in this preface. It's only when you know the system, warts and all, that you can formulate your own strategy for dealing with it. Without such a strategy, you'll have no confidence in what you're doing. You'll be looking anxiously all over the place for clues as to what you should be doing and how. You'll be dragged this way and that, all over the place, trying to keep up. It's like running after a bus, trying to catch it but never quite managing it, tiring yourself out and getting your lungs full of exhaust fumes in the process: a thoroughly frustrating experience.

In this series of student-friendly guides, my overall aim is to help you to take control of your studies, to be confident in what you're doing, and ultimately to get what you want out of your university experience – which I hope will include both fun and having your mind stretched. To this end I have done my best to demystify and make sense of the academic world, to address the many issues which students raise, and to suggest practical courses of action. I've tried to write in plain English, and to help you to deal with academic-speak. Whether you've come to university from school or further education college, or you're a mature student or an international student, I hope these guides will help you to master and enjoy your studies, and to win the qualification you're after.

Peter Levin

Introduction

My aim in writing this Guide is to help you to read and write effectively and efficiently, so that you can write essays that your teachers appreciate and give good marks for, and do so in a way that makes best use of your time and energy.

The culture of higher education in the Western world is very much a culture of the written word. Even in the age of the internet, printed-on-paper books and articles in journals are the prime medium for recording and disseminating thoughts, arguments, research reports, etc., although 'e-journals' are becoming more numerous. Authors commit their message to paper and become publicly identified with what they write. Academics' careers depend on publishing, and counts are made of 'citations', mentions of their publications in someone else's. As a student, if your first question on starting a new course is 'Is there a textbook?', you are in good company: we all feel reassured if we hold the manual in our hands when faced with a new and challenging experience.

Reading and writing at university level are closely connected. Most obviously, when writing essays you will have to draw on materials to be found in books and articles (also known as 'papers' when published in 'learned journals'). But, if you are doing your job properly, the two activities – reading and writing – will also be linked in your own mind. As you think about the subject, your thoughts will provide you with a structured approach to both your reading and your writing, simultaneously. Consider what happens when you're reading and a question comes into your mind. You carry on reading but now you are keeping a lookout for the answer to that question, and you may also now be envisaging that your essay will have a section devoted to that question. Collecting and organizing your thoughts is a central part of both reading and writing.

Here are some of the questions I'm frequently asked about reading and writing:

■ I'm trying to write an essay, and I've got this huge reading list: do I have to read everything? And where do I start?

■ What kind of notes should I take? Is it best to aim to condense the books and articles that I read?

■ I like to begin at the beginning of a book or article and carry on to the end, so I don't miss anything. Isn't that what I'm supposed to do?

■ I'm a very slow reader. How can I read more quickly? Should I take a speed-reading course?

■ When I sit down to read, after a while my mind keeps wandering. I wonder if I'm really suited for academic study: is there any point in my carrying on?

■ I'm told I have to read critically. What does that mean?

■ Some of what I have to read is really hard to understand. Am I stupid?

■ I find it enormously difficult to get started on an essay. I just sit and stare at my computer screen or a blank sheet of paper, sometimes for days. What's wrong with me?

■ I can get started on essays OK, but I never know how to end them. What's the secret?

■ I have to write a 2,000-word essay, I've got heaps of notes, and I've already used 1,000 words on my introduction. What should I do?

■ How should I structure my essays?

■ We've been warned very strongly against plagiarizing, but I'm not clear what I'm supposed not to do. Can you help?

■ I've just had an essay returned with the comment 'You have serious problems with referencing'. This doesn't exactly help me to do better. What do I have to do to get my referencing right?

You'll find answers to all of these questions in this book.

Of course, different people have different abilities, different ways of learning, and different styles of working. I cannot know what *your* particular ones are. I do know from the feedback I get that most of my suggestions work for most people, but you won't necessarily be one of them. And you may already have your own methods that work reasonably well for you and that you don't want to abandon.

So do treat what's in this Guide not as absolute wisdom but as 'worth a try':

see what you can use that works for you. I'm offering you suggestions, not telling you this is how you *must* do it.

It's also the case that different teachers and departments (and faculties and schools) in universities up and down the country have different expectations of students and make different demands of them. Again, I can't be an expert in all of these, and I don't pretend to be. So what I aim to do is to offer you ways of discovering for yourself – by asking questions, by experimenting, by reading between the lines – the expectations and demands that *your* teachers place on you and your fellow students. I aim to help you to become your own expert on how to write for *your* teachers.

Finally, as you may have noticed, this book is the second edition of *Write Great Essays!* It amounts to a complete overhaul of the first edition, published in 2004. It incorporates a great deal of feedback that I have received from students (and a few colleagues). I have rewritten a number of passages where I think I have found a clearer way of expressing what I want to communicate, and others simply because I have had further thoughts. This new edition also addresses some significant developments that have taken place in higher education since 2004: the increasing availability of academic material placed on websites, and a growth in the number of websites offering essays for sale, and, in parallel, a growth in the number of staff, the resources and the technology that institutions are devoting to policing 'plagiarism'. A somewhat strange by-product of the latter is the appearance of a literature on plagiarism, a literature whose authors evidently have academic aspirations. As you will see in the following pages, this literature provides a number of examples of how not to write for an academic audience.

Part 1
Getting started

1

'I'm a slow reader'

Many students tell me they're slow readers. When I ask them how they read, what they actually do when they sit down with a book, it invariably turns out that they take it for granted that they know what 'reading a book' is. It's an activity that consists of beginning to read at page 1 and carrying on until you reach the end at page 250 or whatever, when you've finished. This concept of 'reading' may be psychologically reinforced in a number of ways. You may feel guilty if you skip pages, and if you read the last chapter before you've read all the preceding ones. You may not dare to skip any pages in case you miss something important. And you may feel that 'reading all the way through' is what your teachers – authority figures – expect of you. Not surprisingly, reading the whole book takes a lot of time. And if you find that you never finish the reading before the essay deadline or the class, it can really sap your confidence.

So let's deal with that at the outset. Let me offer you a 'reframe' of your task. Your task is to find in the book those 'bits and pieces' – information, reasoning, ideas, theories, explanations, conclusions – that you want, that will help you to address the topic that has been assigned to you. Think of books as 'treasure chests'. Somewhere inside are the particular gems that you require. You need a quick way of finding them. In this Guide I offer you techniques for doing precisely that.

As for feeling guilty if you don't read every word on every page, bear in mind that the book wasn't written for *you*. Nor was it written with your essay topic in mind. You are under no duty, no obligation, to read it all the way through. And a book of 250 pages contains around 100,000 words: you need to extract from it probably a few hundred at most, less than 1 per cent. Again, your task is not to 'read' the book in the traditional way; your task is to find what is relevant to your needs and to capture it.

Observe how your task is transformed. It's no longer to absorb masses of words, to soak them up like a sponge: rather, it is to do detective work, tracking down what you need. Happily, this is a task that most people's brains enjoy, and are well suited to, whereas soaking up masses of words is not. (If you've ever fallen asleep in a library you'll know what I mean.)

So here's the principle underlying the three 'reading strategies' that I offer in this Guide: be an *active* reader, *interrogate* books, chapters and articles, *use* them to find what is relevant to *your* needs. This is really, really important. Don't be a passive reader, hoping that you'll absorb something from a book if you simply spend enough time with it. It's a forlorn hope: you'll attain nothing more than great depths of boredom.

There are two other factors that might cause you to find reading academic books and articles a very slow, time-consuming activity. One is that you feel obliged to take copious notes, which of course slows down your reading. The trouble is that on a first reading you don't know what is relevant, and consequently you are liable to note – or to highlight – much, much more than you will need.

The second factor that slows down reading is that many academic books and articles are, to all intents and purposes, written in a foreign language, 'academic-speak'. Anthony Giddens, former director of the London School of Economics, told the *Times Higher Education Supplement*: 'I'd spent most of my life writing books for an academic audience, and I used to make these more obscure than they needed to be because that sort of brought you esteem for your scholarship.'[1] This obscurity, deliberate or not, is what you have to contend with. Especially in a subject that is new to you, you have to translate the words on the page from academic-speak into language that you can understand, language that is familiar to you. Again, focusing your efforts on what is relevant to your needs will help you to make this a manageable task.

To sum up: Abandon your preconceived notions of 'reading'. You're in the business of using books and other publications to find what you want. Teach yourself to be a detective. You might even have some fun!

Three stages in academic learning

What should you understand by 'learning'?

Universities promote themselves as institutions of learning. When you first started at university and began your course, was it made crystal clear to you what your teachers meant by 'learning'? If so, you were extremely fortunate. Implicitly, the message that most students get is that learning is what they are expected to supply in between receiving teaching and being examined on what they are taught. That isn't very helpful.

In everyday life, we use the word 'learning' in many different ways. For example, we use it when we mean:

- *memorizing*, like learning your multiplication tables by heart

- *discovering*, like learning something you didn't know before

- *developing skills,* perhaps physical or interpersonal, like learning how to be really good at playing a game or using a piece of equipment or leading a team of people

- *acquiring analytical skills*, like learning how to formulate questions and arrive at answers in the way the experts do

- *acquiring critical skills*, like learning how to test the validity of an argument and 'read between the lines' of government documents and newspaper reports

- *acquiring creative and inventive skills*, like learning to think imaginatively, 'outside the box', and to generate your own ideas

- *making sense*, like learning why something you didn't expect happened, or learning to fathom the motivations behind other people's puzzling behaviour

- *gaining understanding*, like learning how a machine or an organization or a process 'works'

■ *getting a grip on a subject*, like learning everything there is to know about it and being able to talk and write about it in your own words.

In the academic world, your teachers will expect you to learn in all these ways. The precise mixture will depend on what your subject is. For example, if you're studying the humanities your 'learning mix' will not be the same as for students taking a laboratory-based science subject or an applied subject like accountancy or medicine. In subjects where you have to write essays, acquiring analytical, critical and creative skills and generally making sense and gaining understanding are essential if you are to do well. I would sum up your 'learning task' as follows:

Your task is to learn to think for yourself, and to do so in the sort of way that your teachers think. The essays that you write will need to show that you have accomplished this.

Some students find this statement scary. Learning to think for themselves seems an impossible target, and doesn't seem to match up with anything their teachers have told them. But if you look at marking schemes for essays, you will almost always find words such as 'original', 'thoughtful', 'intelligent', 'analytical' and 'imaginative' used to describe top-class work. Work that gets a bare pass or fails is characterized by content that amounts to 'regurgitation' of lecture notes and reading, has a lot of 'padding', and is 'unstructured' and 'predictable': in other words, an absence of thinking for oneself.

Learning to think for yourself is always most difficult when you're just starting. You may feel as though you've been thrown in at the deep end, so to speak, but there are always 'life rafts' to cling on to while you get your bearings, learn the language and begin to recognize what's going on and to find ways of managing.

On the surface, you are at university to learn a subject. You're following a course in sociology, history, law, physics, or whatever. But there's a 'sub-plot': you're also being taught – unconsciously – to think like a sociologist, historian, lawyer, physicist, or whoever. I emphasize the unconscious nature of the process because, in my experience, very few academics are even aware of how they think, let alone set out to teach it. And students who do well pick up their teachers' way of thinking through a similarly unconscious process, a kind of osmosis. But that needn't be the only way. You can learn a lot about how your teachers think by observing them carefully. For example, notice what kind of work they ask you to do: answer a question, solve a problem, or discuss a topic. Then notice their 'methodology': how do they themselves set about answering questions or solving problems or constructing a discussion? I'll come back to this later; for now, just bear in mind that there's a great deal you can do to develop your ability to think for yourself.

I have to stress, though, that there are no short cuts. Please note that academic learning is much more than merely memorizing. Reciting extracts from books, articles, lecture notes or material on the web does not demonstrate that you have learned to think in the way that your teachers think, and may not even get you a pass mark. The same is true of cobbling an essay together by cutting and pasting quotations. And buying an essay that someone else has written and passing it off as your own is a complete no-no. But pay attention to how your teachers think, and you won't be tempted even to consider short cuts like these.

Three stages in academic learning in essay-requiring subjects

If you are taking a subject at university for which essay writing is a major requirement, you will encounter a large amount of written material from which you are expected to 'learn'. What should you actually do?

It seems to me that academic learning in these subjects proceeds in three repeating stages: (1) selecting and copying; (2) translating; and (3) gaining understanding (Table 1). Before you can understand new material you have to translate it into language that makes sense to you, and before you can do this you have to select that material from the deluge that lands on you, and copy it down.

Table 1 Three stages in academic learning

Stage	Activities
Selecting and copying	Making notes
Translating	Paraphrasing and annotating
Gaining understanding	Thinking and reasoning in the subject's language; questioning and evaluating what you read; making connections between material that's new to you and the knowledge you already have; putting concepts and theory together with empirical data, etc.

Selecting and copying

Your academic learning starts from other people's writings and lecturing and from group discussions – in classes, seminars and tutorials. This has important consequences for you. When you're learning something new, you necessarily have to start by selecting and copying other people's work.

You may know this activity as 'making notes': I describe it as *selecting* and *copying* to bring out the fact that you have to select what notes to take. In a lecture you will usually not be able to write down everything the lecturer says: you will try to select what seem to you the most important points, and write those down. Faced with a book, you won't be able to copy out or photocopy the whole book, so you'll try to select relevant passages. But when you first encounter this material you probably won't be in a good position to judge relevance: a common feeling at this point is 'I'll get down as much as I can now, and try to make sense of it later'.

Translating

When you first take notes, the words are of course those of the writer: they still 'belong' to that person. To some extent this is unavoidable, because the subject matter is complex, there are tricky concepts to master, and every subject has its own academic-speak, impenetrable to the newcomer.

What makes matters worse is that much academic writing is poor. Some of it is awful. You are all too likely to come across writers who aren't consistent in the words they use, and who don't offer a decent 'map' to guide the reader through their material. They may fail to make their basic assumptions explicit, and omit steps in their reasoning. You may even encounter some whose command of English grammar, punctuation and sentence structure is weak. And some who produce a torrent not so much of academic-speak as of gobbledygook.

This creates two nuisances that you have to deal with. First, it sets you a bad example and leads you to imitate this style of writing: it's worth making a conscious effort to resist this. Second, when you're reading this stuff it's really hard work to uncover the writer's meaning and reasoning. To make head or tail of it you have to translate it into language that you can understand, that makes sense to you, even if English is your first (or only) language. Indeed, I suspect that all intellectual learning actually involves an 'internal translation' process.

Translating involves expressing the statement on the page in front of you in different words, so you produce an 'equivalent' statement that, all being well, makes sense to you. That is to say, it involves you in *paraphrasing* the original statement. Usually you'll also find yourself *annotating* it: adding clarification, comments, explanations and cross-references.

Gaining understanding

'Gaining understanding' is the next and final stage in academic learning. Now you find yourself increasingly and automatically thinking and reasoning in the subject's language. Perhaps you find yourself appreciating the writer's choice of words and mode of expression, and getting better at detecting relevance and significance in what is written. You'll also find that you are questioning what you read and what you are told: looking for underlying assumptions, seeing whether a conclusion is supported by evidence, disentangling fact from opinion, asking whether a line of reasoning is logical, and so on. You'll be making connections between material that's new to you and the knowledge you already have, looking out for contradictions and 'fit'. And you'll be gaining experience in putting concepts and theory together with empirical data and formulating and testing explanations. In all these ways you'll be learning to see your subject and think about it as your teachers do, all the while learning to do that for yourself rather than just mimicking your teachers.

If you have ever learned a foreign language, you probably had the experience when you started that if someone asked you a question in that language – Spanish, say – you had to translate the question into English, formulate your answer in English, and then translate your answer into Spanish. And then, one day, you were asked a question in Spanish and without a moment's hesitation you gave your answer in Spanish, without going through that intermediate translation process. That is the level of fluency in academic-speak to aim for. When you're there, you'll know it!

When it comes to reading, what are the implications for you of viewing academic learning as this three-stage process: selecting/copying, translating, gaining understanding? For selecting and copying, you need to have some criterion of relevance – importance, significance – for selecting material that you're going to copy into your notes. So you need to start getting some awareness of those criteria as early in your course as you can. For translating purposes, you need to compile a kind of mini-dictionary for yourself, that you can have by you when you read. Again, it helps to start doing this from the beginning. (If you've ever been a language student, you probably kept a vocabulary book for this purpose.) And for the purpose of gaining understanding, you need – I suggest – to start by developing the habit of questioning everything you read and hear. I'll say more about all of these later on.

3

Making notes and translating 'academic-speak'

Students often make heavy weather of making notes and dealing with 'academic-speak'. Here are some suggestions to make life easier for you.

First, so far as making notes is concerned, please resist any urge you might feel to copy out word for word, by hand, large chunks of a book. By doing this you are merely acting as a highly inefficient copying machine. Worse, the material is still the property of the author, so to speak: it hasn't been processed by your mind. You haven't made it 'yours'. Mere copying out is intellectually worthless.

Second, try not to spend hours condensing passages from books. If you do this without any sense of what is relevant among the material, you are again – in my view – largely wasting your time. Condensing is a plodding, brute-force approach to reading matter. It's like looking for pearls by crushing oysters into small bits. Instead, take a pointed knife to your oysters. Look for two or three 'learning points' to take away with you, make a list of the author's main conclusions, capture the 'method, observations, conclusions' or whatever. And don't forget to note where you found these gems, so you can find them again later if you need to.

Third, don't despair if what you find in a book contradicts what you already know, or had thought you knew. If you have made a mistake, this is an opportunity to clear the matter up, and when you have done so you will know this bit of your subject better than before. And sometimes you will find a genuine disagreement between authors. Excellent! This is an opportunity to learn the skill of critical reading. Try to track down the source of the disagreement. For example, is it a difference in assumptions or beliefs, or in the data used, or in methods of analysis? And when you have tracked down the source of the disagreement, try to form your own judgment as to who is right or who you agree with. Judge for yourself if someone has made an unwarranted inference or logical error. If you're not confident about this, ask your teachers for help. They should be intrigued by problems like these that involve detective work.

Don't expect critical reading to come easily. It takes experience. Finding and reading books by more than one author on the same subject and exploring the disagreements between them is a good way of gaining that experience.

Fourth, if you're starting a new subject you'll certainly find it reassuring to have a textbook that covers the whole course, or, failing that, to be pointed to a short introductory book or a review article or two. That's OK for starters, but such 'potted' treatments do little to help you to develop your reasoning in the subject, and in many cases they are inadequate as sources of quotations. So get into the habit of checking out the original sources that they draw on. Apart from anything else, this will help to alert you to the limitations and deficiencies that are to be found in secondary sources, and thereby further develop your critical reading skills.

Fifth, don't expect academic books and articles to be easy to understand when you first open them and start reading. Being written in academic-speak, they'll need translating into language you comprehend. Especially if your first language is not English, this won't be easy at first. But don't be disheartened, and don't let the author make you feel stupid or inadequate. Work steadily through the text, paragraph by paragraph, sentence by sentence, and – if necessary – word by word. Bit by bit you will master the language, and you'll find that in the process you've also acquired the skill of thinking critically.

In Box 1 I've provided an illustration of the painstaking (and sometimes painful) work that translating academic writing calls for. I have selected a passage on the subject of 'plagiarism' taken from an article by P. J. Larkham entitled 'Exploring and dealing with plagiarism: traditional approaches' which (at the time of writing) is available on the Plagiarism Advisory Service website.[1] In the left-hand column I have reproduced the original: in the right-hand column is my attempt to make sense of it.

Box 1 Translating academic-speak

What is plagiarism? (A)	**(A)** The question: 'What is plagiarism?'
Hawley (1984) views plagiarism as being a continuum (**B**) ranging from sloppy paraphrasing to verbatim transcription with no crediting of sources: indeed, 'definitional precision constitutes one of the most salient problems in any discussion of acceptable versus unacceptable documentation' (Hawley, 1984, p. 35). It is this variability that produces problems in attempting to	implies that there is something that plagiarism *is*, an activity or behaviour which everyone recognizes as such when they see it. But 'plagiarism' is a word – a label – to which different people attach different meanings. It would be better to ask: 'What is meant by "plagiarism"?' To fail to put the word in quotes is to confuse the label with the activity, the description with the actuality.

'prove' many instances of alleged plagiarism, and seeking to apply appropriate sanctions. Nevertheless, a strong similarity between two texts remains *prima facie* evidence of plagiarism. Brownlee (1987) has suggested that the major problem surrounding plagiarism (**C**) is not that of misunderstandings of the mechanics of scholarship or documentation (although many, e.g. McCormick, 1989; Nienhuis, 1989, (**D**) feel that it is), but one of the practice of scholarship (**E**), especially where students are under time pressures while needing to review literature and formulate their own ideas. It is possible that changes to more continuous assessment and away from reliance on traditional unseen examinations have exacerbated the problem: and some universities are deliberately moving back to requiring each module to comprise at least 50 per cent examination assessment in response.

Scollon (1995) takes issue with these 'traditional' views of plagiarism. (**F**) He rightly suggests (**G**) that this type of view implies much about the nature of discourse, the person(s) communicating, and the (private or individual) 'ownership' of discourse. In particular, communication – including issues involving plagiarism – is 'a cultural model which can be located in terms of a particular historical moment and a particular cultural group' (Scollon, 1995, p. 5; and see Howard, 2000, (**H**) for a discussion on Western theories of authorship). Scollon views this as developing into a particular economic/ ideological system, that of Europe at the time of the Enlightenment, and a particular view of authors as manufacturers of texts but texts as commercial products. This ideological

(**B**) '[Views] plagiarism as being a continuum'. I think Larkham means that Hawley has identified a range of plagiarizing activities which can be arranged on a kind of 'acceptability' scale.

(**C**) '[The] major problem surrounding plagiarism'. If the 'surrounding' metaphor baffles you, try 'The major problem associated with plagiarism'.

(**D**) You might want to question whether a mere two examples support the assertion that 'many . . . feel', and how what an author feels can be inferred from what he or she writes.

(**E**) In relaying Brownlee's suggestion 'that the major problem . . . is . . . one of the practice of scholarship', Larkham is telling us something *about* the problem but not what he sees the problem *as*. Perhaps we should translate the suggestion as: 'Students are particularly prone to commit plagiarism because they are untutored in the practice of scholarship, hence the problem is how to provide that tutoring.'

(**F**) What 'traditional' views? The only 'view' put forward thus far is Hawley's of 'plagiarism as a continuum'. We can only guess what Larkham means by ' "traditional" views of plagiarism'.

(**G**) 'Scollon . . . rightly suggests': an alternative wording would be 'Scollon suggests, and I agree with him'. Notice how Larkham's wording disguises the fact that the opinion expressed is that of himself alone: his wording makes the opinion seem more authoritative. Translate this as: 'Larkham agrees with Scollon's suggestion.'

(**H**) Larkham does not give page or chapter references to Howard's book, nor system (**I**) values particular concepts, (**J**) including individual autonomy, rationality, originality and objectivity (Scollon, 1995; Lanham, 1983). Of course, the universities experiencing problems of plagiarism are strongly rooted in this particular ethic and milieu. (**K**)

There are, however, various value-sets which do not regard plagiarism as an issue (**L**) – and certainly not as a problem. (**M**) This is particularly true of some creative arts (cf. Randall, 2001). (**N**)

to some other books mentioned. A student could lose marks for doing this.

(**I**) Observe how 'economic/ideological system' has become transmuted into 'ideological system'. Perhaps we have to treat these terms as interchangeable.

(**J**) I have difficulty with 'This ideological system values particular concepts'. Perhaps we should translate it as: 'People who subscribe to or are caught up in this system value individual autonomy, etc.'

(**K**) '*Which* particular ethic and milieu?' Larkham is introducing new terms here. My translation is: 'The ethic and milieu associated with this ideological (or economic/ideological) system'.

(**L**) I suppose the statement 'various value-sets . . . do not regard . . .' has to be translated as 'there are people who subscribe to other values who do not regard . . .'.

(**M**) What's the difference between an 'issue' and a 'problem'? Is a problem more urgent?

(**N**) No page or chapter references are given for Randall's book. 'cf.' is short for the Latin word *confer*, which in English means compare. Larkham doesn't say why we should compare what he writes with what Randall writes. Are we meant to infer that Randall supports him?

Sixth, it is always worthwhile to check out the structure of a publication. A while ago, a student showed me an article which he had been struggling to understand. A quick inspection revealed that there was a statement of the article's aims in the Abstract; another, *different,* statement of aims in the Introduction; and a third statement of aims, *different again*, in the Conclusions. And while the title of the article posed a question, the Conclusions did not contain the answer to it! It was not surprising that the student had been struggling to understand the article. His difficulty didn't arise from lack of ability on his part: it arose because the article was a poor piece of work. If you are told to read something which you find to be as badly organized as this example, go back to your teacher and ask: 'What are the two or three learning points that I should take from this?' If you don't get a helpful answer, it may be best to spend no more time on it.

Seventh, my attitude to academic reading is that what you need is an eye for relevance and the ability to translate and make sense of what you read. Speed is not crucial: 100 per cent comprehension of important material *is*.

A word here about 'speed-reading' and 'photo-reading' techniques. 'Speed reading' and 'photo reading' are not reading in the sense that you are accustomed to, a speeded-up version of what you normally do. They are techniques for mentally photographing pages of print – installing them in your subconscious mind – and accessing relevant material on demand. The reading strategies that I advocate in this book do make some use of them – the books that I have drawn on are listed in the 'Books on Speed Reading' section at the end of this book – but because I have found them of limited help when it comes to translating and comprehending academic-speak I have made some adaptations.

But you may have some bad reading habits that slow you down. If you read aloud, or voice the words under your breath, you are limiting your reading speed to your speaking speed, which is far slower. And if you focus on one word at a time, your eyes are moving along each line of text in a series of jumps rather than smoothly. Speed-reading techniques can help you get out of these bad habits. Do a Google search for 'speed reading' and check out the various systems – starting with those offering free trials – for one that you feel comfortable with. Such techniques may give your eyes some useful training, so that you 'see' two or three lines at a time, rather than only one word.

Eighth, a word of warning about 'course packs'. You may be able to buy – or even be given – a collection of off-prints, usually photocopied articles and chapters from books. Be very wary about relying on the latter. A 'middle' chapter from a book, unless it is a 'free-standing' chapter from an edited, multi-author book, has been taken out of context, and you may be missing a great deal by not seeing that context. So if you're told such a chapter is important to read, try to get hold of the book itself and look through at least the first and last chapters. In my experience, students who have done this have almost always found it worthwhile.

4

Coping with monster reading lists

If you have been issued with 'monster' reading lists, you have my sympathy. Such lists can be hugely intimidating, especially when you first encounter them. But there are ways of getting to grips with them.

First of all, though, a question: what makes a reading list long? There can be several explanations. Many teachers are well aware that the demand to borrow books from the library always exceeds the supply, and so they may well include two or more books that cover the same ground – especially if it's basic material – to maximize the likelihood that you and your fellow-students will find that material somewhere. Clearly you don't need to read *all* the books that cover that ground. So if the list includes a number of basic texts, one will usually be sufficient. (Refer to a second one if there's something in the first that you feel you need to check or clarify.) It's best to use what time you have to cover a variety of reading.

A list may also be long because the teacher who compiled it intended it to be a comprehensive list of references on the subject, to be used by students as a source of materials for in-depth essays or preparing for exams, as well as for seminar preparation. In this case the list ought to be divided into 'essential reading' (for seminars) and 'further reading' (for more advanced work), but this isn't always done. If it *is* done, concentrate on the essential reading first: if it *isn't* done, ask your teacher for advice.

And a list may be long because teachers have added new items as they have been published, but not weeded out old ones. Books or journal articles more than ten or twenty years old (it'll vary from subject to subject) and that aren't classics may well have been superseded by more recent publications. My advice is to start with the most recent ones. Not only will they be more up to date, but they may also include summaries and critiques of the earlier material and may have more comprehensive lists of references. If your reading list doesn't include the dates of publication of books, ask your teacher to supply them. Failing that, look them up in your library's online catalogue.

Finally, keep your eye on the assessment ball. You need reading lists not only so that you can write essays and participate in seminars but also so that later on you can write assessed essays and revise for unseen (traditional) exams. To write an unassessed essay early in the year you don't need to have made yourself an expert on the topic. Read three or four items. Identify significant conclusions and problematic issues and questions and write about those. That will move your learning on, and give you a basis to build on later.

Part 2

Reading purposes and strategies

5

What are you reading for?

It is really important, before you start reading a book, chapter or article, that you are clear in your mind *why* you are reading it, what you are reading it *for*. If you are reading aimlessly, the chances are that you will soon find yourself just idly turning the pages, then gazing at them without making sense of the words while your mind is somewhere else entirely. So whenever you start reading something, pause and ask yourself: Why am I doing this? What do I want to get out of it? What is my task, what's the job I have to do?

Note that 'because it's on my reading list' is not *by itself* a sufficient reason for starting to read something. (Nor, indeed, is 'my teacher told me to'.) You really do need to have a specific *purpose*. There has to be something that you want to get from your reading.

You can read for different purposes and in different ways. In Table 2 I list three reading strategies – 'exploratory', 'dedicated' and 'targeted' – together with the task to which that particular kind of reading is suited.

It may be that you are sometimes so grabbed by something you are reading that you just can't put it down, and don't want to even though it's three in the morning. I won't tell you to resist that compulsion. But you have a lot of work to do, and you must make best use of your limited time. Accordingly, I am concentrating here on exploratory, dedicated and targeted reading. If there's a book that really grabs you, and you want to read it just for interest and pleasure, save it as a treat: make it a reward for yourself when you've just handed in an essay or given a presentation.

Table 2 Three reading strategies and their application to essay writing

Strategy	Task to which this strategy is suited
'Exploratory' reading	1. Getting an overview – a bird's-eye view – of a text. Useful for working your way quickly through items on a reading list and identifying sections or passages that *might* be useful for your essay. Worth doing when you start work on an assignment 2. Casting around, especially on the web, for items that are not on your reading list. Useful for widening your knowledge and checking your sources. Worth doing once you have gained your overview, and could impress your teachers
'Targeted' reading	When you have identified from your overview a section or passage that might be useful, focusing on it for a closer look, and (if you decide it *will* be useful) working through it thoroughly. Essential if you are to get good marks
'Dedicated' reading	Working your way through a textbook or set text which you are required to master. Useful for getting on top of a subject and mastering essential language and concepts

6

Exploratory reading (1): How to get an overview

'Exploratory' reading is what you do if you want to get an overview of a text (a book, chapter or article): to make a summary of it, or gain an overall appreciation of it – a bird's-eye view. You're aiming to get a sense of it without going into detail. It's like making a map of a forest without recording every tree in it. It's a helpful thing to do when you're starting out in a new field of study, or if your teacher has asked you to write a review of a book that's new to you. It's particularly useful if you need to work your way quickly through items on a reading list to identify potentially useful passages in them.

Exploratory reading for an essay topic should begin with the reading list you've been given. You might like to re-read Chapter 4, 'Coping with monster reading lists'. This should help you not to be intimidated by the length of a list and give you a start in focusing on what you actually need.

What should you do with your reading list? First, you should do the obvious thing: look to see how much guidance it gives you. If good practice has been followed, you should be able to answer yes to all the following questions:

- Has your teacher 'starred' any items as essential reading, or divided the list into two parts, such as 'Main Reading' and 'Further Reading', or books and articles?

- Are particular chapters or pages recommended?

- Does the list give the year of publication of books?

- If books are collections of chapters or articles by different people – these books should be shown as having editors rather than authors – have particular chapters been picked out as more relevant to your needs?

Try to get hold of everything that is listed as essential or main reading, and of as many as possible of the most up-to-date items: these are most likely to have the fullest range of further references to follow up. (Even if a book that you need is being used by someone else, go to the shelf where it should be and see if there are other books nearby that you can use.) And if there are several basic texts on a reading list, one – or at most two – will usually be sufficient for writing an essay.

Now you need an overview of each of the essential and recent publications. To do this, I suggest that you follow the steps set out in Table 3.

Table 3   Six steps in overviewing

Step	Task
1	See what type of publication you are faced with
2	Get acquainted with the structure of the publication
3	Notice clues to the author's approach
4	Find out what you can about the author's conclusions
5	'Map' the publication (optional)
6	Compile your overview

Step 1: See what type of publication you are faced with

When you first open something you haven't read before, it is always a good idea to try to get some idea of the *type* of publication it is. In Table 4 I have listed some of the commonly encountered types (and you can see what I mean by 'type' from the contents of the list), together with some key words which will help you to recognize them.

So what should you do? If the publication is a book, take a look through the foreword (if there is one), the preface (if there is one), the introduction and/or chapter 1, and the final chapter. In the case of a self-contained chapter or article, check out the abstract, the opening section and the concluding section. Don't actually go through this material word by word and line by line: instead, just run your eyes over it, keeping a lookout for the key words listed in the right-hand column of Table 4. It won't take a lot of practice before you'll be able to tell at a glance what type of publication you're looking at.

Table 4 Types of publication

Type	Brief description	Key words
'Q to A' (Question to Answer)	Starts with a question and concludes with the answer to it. Answers range from plausible speculation to rigorous explanation in terms of theories and mechanisms	Question, answer, reasoning; puzzle, solution; phenomenon, situation, event, behaviour; explain, explanation, account for, evidence, observations, conditions; process, mechanism; theory
Research report	The story of what the author did and found	Investigation, case study; objective, hypothesis; method/methodology, evidence, observations; analysis, results, findings, significance, conclusions
Theory	Presents a conceptual framework of some kind and its implications	Theory, concept, assumptions, model, variables, cause and effect; describe, explain, connect, integrate, relate; words ending in 'ism'
Argument/ critique of argument	Argues/puts the case for or against a particular proposition or point of view	Argue, argument, thesis, case, proposition; attack, critique; objections, refutations; valid, invalid; true, false; correct, incorrect
Issue-centred/ advocacy	Starts with an issue (a 'What should be done?' question) and usually concludes by advocating a particular course of action	Issue, problem, question, dilemma, difficulty; solution, proposal, recommendation, course of action; should, ought, must; beliefs; right, wrong; costs, benefits; beneficial, harmful; fair, unfair: appropriate, inappropriate
Review	Surveys and discusses research findings, theories, arguments, issues, etc. in a systematic way	Review, literature review, survey, 'state of the art', debate
Theme-based	Is constructed around a theme and incorporates elements of some or all of the above	Theme, aspects; explore, discuss, consider, look at; contribute to the debate
Textbook	A compilation of some or all of the above, tailored to a student readership	

The value of this exercise lies in helping you to 'get your head round' a text: you've taken the first step towards making good use of it and selecting out parts that you can safely disregard. An incidental benefit is that you will quickly be reminded that many – possibly all – of the items on your reading lists were not written with you or your essay in mind.

Step 2: Get acquainted with the structure of the publication

By the 'structure' of the publication I mean the way it is organized, laid out. To get acquainted with it, here are some questions to ask yourself, and some suggestions for things you can do:

- If the publication is a book, take a look at the contents page or pages. How informative are the chapter headings in the contents list? How much do they tell you? Can you discern a logic to the sequence of chapters? (Can you see a rationale that led the author to put them in that order rather than a different one?) Are the chapters grouped into 'parts', and do these have helpful headings?

- Turn to the preface (if there is one) and the introduction (which may or may not be labelled 'Chapter 1') and look for descriptions of what's in the individual chapters. Look out for expressions such as 'In chapter 2 I examine . . .' and 'The third chapter deals with . . . I then go on to consider . . .'. Then check these against the chapter headings in the contents list. Do this by writing out the contents list, or by making a photocopy, and annotating it, to give yourself a list of chapters with fuller descriptions than the contents page provides.

  NB The habit of cross-checking, which encompasses cross-referencing and testing for consistency, is one of the most useful habits that you can develop as a reader. If you detect inconsistencies (including inconsistencies in the way that a particular word is used), be very, very wary. If you can't trust the author to write clearly, you can't trust him or her to think clearly either.

- Are the chapters split into sections, and, if so, are the headings of the sections shown in the contents list? If they aren't, go through the chapters one by one, making your own contents list for each. It's simple to do, and can be very revealing.

- If the publication is a self-contained chapter or an article, it won't have a contents list, so it is particularly important that you make your own. Go through it making a list of headings, sub-headings and sub-sub-headings. I'd be surprised if you don't find this extremely helpful. For example, you may be able to see immediately which sections you should read first and which you can save for later or leave out altogether.

■ Where are the publication's conclusions? Is there actually a chapter or section called 'Conclusions'? If not, and there often isn't, you have to play a game called 'hunt the conclusions'. They might be in the final sections of intermediate chapters; or they might be in the preface or introduction. (This is especially likely if the publication is of the theory or advocacy type.)

■ Look for links between chapters and sections. A good place to look is the first and last paragraphs. In the first paragraph, look for a form of words such as: 'In the previous chapter/section we saw . . .'. In the last paragraph, look for a form of words such as: 'In the next chapter/section . . .' When you come to the final chapter of a book, skim through it looking for references to previous chapters. If there are none, you really should ask what the connection is between that chapter and the earlier ones.

Step 3: Notice clues to the author's approach

Begin by reminding yourself what type of publication it is that you're working on (see Table 4). Then, if the publication is a book, take a closer look this time at the foreword, preface, introduction and/or chapter 1, and the final chapter. In the case of a self-contained chapter or article, take a closer look at the abstract, the opening section and the concluding section. Then do the following:

■ Ask yourself what this book is for? Who is it for? Indeed, why did the author take the trouble to write it?

■ Look for statements of purpose or objectives and check whether they are consistent with one another. Notice whether the author is sharing with you his or her 'vision' of the book. Pay particular attention not only to the earlier chapters or sections but also to the concluding ones: it is quite usual to find objectives restated in a book's final chapter or an article's final section, and they may take a form that is different from earlier statements. (Often it's here that you'll find the clearest and most succinct description of the author's objectives, possibly because it was only when he or she came to write their conclusions that they had fully clarified what they were doing.)

■ With a publication of the 'Q to A' type, make a note of the question(s) and the answer(s). Note the event, situation, behaviour or whatever it is that the question refers to, and the mode of reasoning used to get from question to answer. Does the author tell a story? Refer to 'factors'? Use 'counterfactual' ('what if?') reasoning? Does the answer have to be merely 'plausible'? Or does the author attempt a rigorous explanation, exposing the mechanisms at work and citing consistency with evidence and theory as the test of a good answer? Look carefully at the language the author uses, and check whether a word is used with the same meaning throughout, and whether different words are used as synonyms (i.e. treated as having the same meaning).

■ With a 'research report', write a short note listing the author's objectives, methodology (method of working), results/findings and conclusions. There are two points to make here: (1) conclusions are almost always based on an interpretation of results, so look closely at how the author has done this interpreting; and (2) exploratory reading doesn't require you to have a detailed grasp of the author's methodology, so don't spend a lot of time on this unless you are told to.

■ With a publication that presents a 'theory', your first task must be to make sure you grasp the meanings of the words used. It might help to make a little glossary – a list of words and their meanings – for yourself. With a book, go through the index at the back, identify words and phrases that you're not familiar with, and look up their meanings. That done, there are three useful questions you can ask for the purpose of exploratory reading: (1) What does the author say this theory, model or whatever does? (Look for the words 'explain', 'connect', 'integrate', 'relate', 'describe'.) (2) What does the author say about the assumptions or premises on which the theory is based? (3) What does the author say about how the validity and usefulness of the theory can be tested?

■ A publication of the 'argument/critique of argument' type will usually start by setting out the point or proposition over which there is debate or dis-agreement, or the position which is being attacked, and the author's own position. The remainder will often take a series of grounds for disagree-ment, one by one. Note the author's own position and his or her grounds for disagreeing with others.

■ With a publication of the 'issue-centred/advocacy' type, there are several things to do. Look for a clear statement of the issue: this may be buried in a review of the history or literature, and need to be unearthed. Get clear in your mind what the 'solution' is that the author is advocating. Look for assumptions on which the solution is based: these often need to be unearthed, but may well be open to questioning. Find the 'imperative' words ('should', 'ought', 'must', etc.) and the 'value judgment' words ('good', 'bad', etc.) and note whether these occur throughout or only towards the end in deriving the solution. How far does the author go in attempting to justify those imperatives and value judgments? (Do they turn out to rest on something more than appeals to common sense and good nature?)

■ With a publication of the 'review' type, exploratory reading will often require you to do no more than gain a grasp of the author's conclusions. So I suggest you don't read anything else, unless, again, you are told to, in which case ask why.

■ With a publication of the 'theme-based' type, you may well feel that you're looking at a collage, a patchwork of bits and pieces of 'pure' elements: 'Q to A', research report, theory, and so on. Publications of this type, especially books, can be very difficult to get your head round. They're rather like a chest of drawers into which clothes have been stuffed without being sorted. The language used is often 'high' academic-speak: 'woolly' and unspecific. Characteristically, themes are not stated with the clarity and precision of a question, a phenomenon or a proposition. And authors use terms such as 'explore', 'discuss', 'consider' and 'look at', rather than 'ask' and 'test'. The only obvious guide that you have to the author's approach is the chapter headings and what he or she tells you about their approach in the introductory and concluding chapters/sections. It may be worth doing a little digging, however. If the author claims to be exploring a subject, see if there are any clues as to how he or she 'does' exploring. Try to avoid going into too much detail, however: this is only exploratory reading, remember.

If you're lucky, the heading to a chapter will tell you which particular aspect of the theme is dealt with in that chapter. If you aren't lucky, and the headings are quirky, metaphorical or merely numbers, read the first and last paragraphs for clues as to the subject matter of the chapter. And see what you can glean from reading through the index, if there is one. Terms with the largest number of page entries, whether these cluster together or are widely spread, may well be the themes that have preoccupied the author.

■ In a well-organized 'textbook', irrespective of the elements that it contains, you should find informative chapter headings and the structure of the book already mapped out for you. You may be expected to work steadily through the book from beginning to end, or to use it as a reference book, cross-checking with material that you get in lectures. If it is not already done for you, list the chapter sub-headings as well as the headings themselves, and make sure you know what each refers to. That will usually be sufficient for exploratory reading.

Step 4: Find out what you can about the author's conclusions

Conclusions can take many forms. For example, the conclusions to a research report could include the explanation put forward for the author's findings, a statement about the need for further research, reflections on the methodology employed, and a discussion of the significance and wider implications of the findings. Having tracked down the author's conclusions, ask yourself:

■ What kinds of conclusions did the author reach? What are they about? Do I really need to know about all of them? If the answer is no, asking this question could save you quite a lot of work.

    NB Don't have any qualms about skipping to the final chapter or chapters without first reading the intervening ones. You are under absolutely no obligation to plough through the whole thing. Unless the book is a novel, it really isn't cheating to look at the ending. Indeed, the end of a book is usually a brilliant vantage point for looking back and picking out the author's train of thought.

■ If the conclusions are scattered through the publications, when viewed together are they consistent with one another?

■ How do the author's conclusions relate to the objectives set out in the preface, introduction or chapter 1 (in the case of a book) or in the abstract and opening section in the case of a chapter or article? For example, if the author started off with a question, does he or she conclude by restating that question and providing the answer? If the book was intended to be a survey of a field, does the final chapter present an overview? If the article was intended to be a discussion of a theme, does the final section bring different aspects together and present a coherent summing-up?

    Note that not all publications have conclusions. This is particularly likely for the 'theory' and 'theme-based' types, some of which may strike you – as they do me – as barely structured outpourings of the author's mind. If you have been struggling with a book (say) of this kind, try this. Without looking at it, sit yourself somewhere comfortable, imagine you're having a coffee with a friend, and imagine that your friend is asking you: 'What do you think are the two or three main points that it's worth taking from this book?' Don't stress yourself: just relax, take a clean sheet of paper, and write down whatever comes into your head. (This will probably work even better if you really do go and have coffee with a friend and your friend really does ask you that question.) Then go and see the teacher who recommended the book to you, and ask him or her the same question. The fact that you have made an effort may be conducive to getting a helpful answer.

Step 5: 'Map' the publication (optional)

Mapping is about identifying for yourself the various parts or 'building blocks' of the publication and the connections between those building blocks, and showing the blocks and connections in diagrammatic form. Many people find such diagrams helpful, but not everybody does. If you feel that you belong to the latter group, feel free to skip this step.

You have already done some of this work in steps 1–4, when you familiarized yourself with the publication's type and layout and found out what you could about the author's approach. Now it's time to concentrate on the links.

To start, take as blocks the chapters and/or sections, i.e. blocks as the author has created them. A connection, or link, exists between two such blocks when the later one *draws on* the earlier one in some way or is a *logical sequel* to it. Thus in an account of research framed to test an hypothesis, you will almost certainly find that the description of the work carried out draws on the hypothesis formulated in an earlier chapter, that the report of the results *refers back* to the description of the work carried out, that when discussing the significance of results the author *picked out* certain of those results.

In effect, what you are doing here is describing the links between blocks in terms of a *physical action or relationship* of some kind. Here are some more examples:

■ The methodology *is based on* the hypothesis that . . .

■ In the conclusions, the author returns to the question posed at the outset, so the book *comes full circle* . . .

■ The discussion *brings together* . . .

- These assumptions *lead to* the conclusion that . . .

- There are three *successive stages* in the author's argument . . .

- Each of the case studies *is self-contained* . . .

With a little practice it should be fairly straightforward to show in dia-grammatic form each of the relationships or dynamics that you find. Lines, arrow heads and boxes are the only tools you need.

Get yourself a large sheet of paper: flipchart paper is best, whichever way up you prefer. Start with a rough draft. Pick out any sequence of blocks that seems to be obvious and draw connecting lines between them (use arrow-heads if there's an obvious directionality) to represent the links: this will give you a kind of spine to your map. Then work out how the other blocks connect (or don't) to this spine. Put in each link by drawing a line between the two connected blocks. Carry on doing this until all the links that you have iden-tified are shown. If there are any unconnected blocks left, show these by 'islands' towards the edge of your sheet of paper. When all the blocks and links are shown, hey presto! You have your map!

The 'shape' of your map has some important messages for you. If it consists entirely of islands, don't waste your time trying to invent links (but do check with your teacher in case you have overlooked something important, and while you're about it ask why this book has been commended to you). If there are just a few islands, those blocks are evidently not part of the 'mainstream' of the author's exposition, and for the purposes of exploratory reading you can probably safely ignore them.

Sometimes you will also see that certain parts of the book did *not* con-tribute to the conclusions – they aren't actually mentioned in the final chapter – and you will be able to ignore these or leave them until later.

If your map is basically a line of links – a chain of blocks from 'background' to 'conclusion', say – with other links connecting to blocks at the sides, you need to use arrows to show whether those blocks are 'feeding into' the main chain or 'branching off'. If the latter, note their presence, but don't pay too much attention to them. They are literally side issues. Concentrate on the main chain and the blocks that feed into it.

Bear in mind that in writing a book an author is constrained by two needs: the need to force his or her material into a linear, chapter-by-chapter pro-gression, and the need to present it in a way that the reader can assimilate. If the book is an original piece of work, you can be absolutely certain that the author's thought process was complicated and far from linear: more akin to doing a jigsaw puzzle where the picture is blurred, many of the pieces are missing, and there are no straight edges or right-angled corners. As a result you may sometimes find that some of your links form a loop, with all the arrowheads pointing clockwise or anticlockwise. Such loops may be interesting to pursue later.

Finally: mapping a book is a good way of 'capturing' on a single sheet of paper what the author is presenting and – more important – those blocks that will be of relevance to you in your studies. The map is also a visual aid: preparing it and subsequently looking at it will help to fix your overview of the book in your memory. With practice, you should be able to create a map of a book of 250 pages in 30 or 40 minutes and form your own view of its value to you.

Step 6: Compile your overview

Compiling your overview is basically a matter of putting together – assembling – the notes you made in steps 1–4, possibly adding any thoughts that have occurred to you while making your map. So it could be divided into five sections:

- Type of publication. Give factual details (e.g. title, author, date of publication, publisher), note its type from Table 4, and add any thoughts you've had about it.

- Structure of the publication. Describe briefly how it is organized: how it is divided into parts and how they fit together. If you've made a map it will come in useful here. Make a note of how easy (or not) you found it to grasp the structure, and of any complications or omissions you have found.

- The author's approach. Say what you have discovered about the author's objectives and methods, and again add any relevant comments you may have, including a comment as to whether it is suited to the audience for which the author intended it.

- The author's conclusions. Again, say what you have discovered. Refer back to step 4 for the points you could include here.

- The main points that you take from the publication, and how it helps you in studying the subject.

7

Exploratory reading (2): How to use the World Wide Web

There is more than one way of going about preparing to write an essay. You can restrict yourself to the material that's on the reading list you've been given. If you work your way systematically through it you'll probably have done a good enough job. But, if time allows, you can be a bit more enterprising and indeed more inventive. You can use a search engine to cast your net more widely. Here's an illustration.

Let's say you have an essay to write on the subject of 'moral panics'. You've probably been given a reading list but you want to investigate what else there is around. How could a search engine help?

Let's use Google, which is said to be 'the most popular search engine [among] savvy web users'.[1] Open your internet browser. Type the phrase "moral panic" (no need for the plural) into the 'search box', the box to the left of the Search button. Be sure to include the phrase between the double quotation marks, otherwise Google will search for pages where the two words occur singly as well as together.

Then click on the Google Search button (next to the search box). This will take you to another Google page that comprises a list of ten web pages. In the top right-hand corner of the page you will see 'Results 1–10 of about 438,000 for "moral panic"'. (All these results totals were found on 29 January 2009, and I give them here as an illustration. They could be quite different at the time you are reading this.) Of course, 438,000 references to 'moral panic' is rather more than you want. So, while you're at the top of the page, underneath the search box click on the radio button (the little half-shaded circle) by the words 'pages from the UK'. You'll see that the results are down to about 67,500. An improvement, but nowhere near good enough.

Now remember that you're engaged on an academic piece of work. So it could be helpful to concentrate on pages from academic sources. Do this by typing something extra into the search box, the term "ac.uk", which will filter out pages from non-academic sources. Search again. Now you're down to about 11,800 results. Definitely better, but still capable of being improved on.

Go the bottom of the Google page that you're on. (Either scroll down or press the Page Down [PgDn] key on your computer.) Click on the little 10 that you'll see there. This will take you to another page showing results 91–100. Go to the bottom of this page and click on the little 19. Now you see results 181–190. Down to the bottom again, click on the little 28. This gets you to results 271–280. Repeat the process, and click on the little 37, and you find results 361–370. Repeat once more, click on the little 46, and you have results 451–460. Click on the little 55, and you have results 541–550. Now click on the little 64: this gives you results 631–640, but at the foot of the page there's nothing to click on beyond the little 66. Click on this, and you find you're on a page with results 641–647. At the foot is the message: 'In order to show you the most relevant results, we have omitted some entries very similar to the 647 already displayed.' So you have reduced the original 438,000 results to 647. Now your task is beginning to approach manageable proportions.

(NB You can speed up this process considerably by telling Google to show you as many as 100 results on a single page. Click on Preferences next to the Search button, and you'll be invited to choose to have 20, 30, 50 or 100 results displayed at a time.)

As you look down the list of web pages that are offered to you, you'll begin to see that they are of a few distinct kinds. There are some that you can – and should – simply not bother to open: course prospectuses and essay questions in which 'moral panic' (or 'moral panics', plural) is mentioned, advertisements for lectures in which the speaker will touch on 'moral panics'; most blogs, whether by academics or students; pages that refer to but are not actually part of an ac.uk site; PowerPoint pages (these have the suffix 'ppt'); abstracts of articles as opposed to the complete publication.

Which pages *are* worth opening and looking at? You will find some pages containing papers that have previously been published on paper in specialist journals and that have been refereed, which gives them some authority. These papers are usually on the web in pdf form (portable document format), so you can read them but not copy from them (unless you have specialist software). They are easy to recognize: the last three letters of the web address are 'pdf'. You will probably find some 'working papers' produced by academic research institutes: they probably won't have been refereed but should have been read and commented on by the authors' colleagues. And you will find some materials created by academics or course teams for their own students: you can expect these too to be authoritative, and there is no reason why you shouldn't look at them and learn from them. You will also find some essays written by students which their teachers have deemed worth publishing on the web. These may be worth looking at for ideas and sources, but they will carry no weight with your own teachers – they won't be regarded as authoritative – so you should definitely not spend a lot of time on them.

However, at the very top of Google's 647-strong list is a web page that comprises an essay entitled 'What are "moral panics"?' by one Hayley Burns and dated April 2000.[2] This seems to be a student essay, but there is nothing on the page itself to say who Hayley Burns is, what course she was taking, what year she was in, or even what institution she was studying at. We can find something more by truncating the web address (see endnote),[3] which takes us to a page headed 'The Media and Communications Studies Site' hosted by Aberystwyth University. Under the heading 'Directory: Student Essays', the author of this page refers to 'my own courses' and 'my own students' – so Hayley Burns was evidently a student at Aberystwyth – but does not give his or her own name. All very unsatisfactory.

Once we've found a seemingly relevant web page, what do we look for? A good place to start is definitions. In the second paragraph of her essay, Hayley Burns writes: 'It was Stanley Cohen, in his work *Folk Devils and Moral Panics* (1987) who first coined the term[4] "moral panics".' And she goes on to offer Cohen's definition of the term and description of its characteristics, although she puts only the latter within quotation marks.

Now let's step back a bit. A place to look for definitions is a dictionary or encyclopaedia. At the very top of the biggest list (438,000 entries) that Google produced for us was Wikipedia, the free encyclopedia. Wikipedia gets a lot of stick from academics, and you may have been advised not to touch it, but it can be very helpful. Clicking on this link takes us to the relevant web page.[5] And here we read: 'While many believe the term was coined by Stanley Cohen . . . it was actually first used by his colleague Jock Young when he used it in reference to the reaction to drug takers in Notting Hill.' As one would hope there's a footnote at this point, but – illustrating the imperfection of Wikipedia – it refers not to Jock Young's original publication but to a secondary source, an A-level Sociology textbook, *Mass Media*, by Marsha Jones and Emma Jones, published by Macmillan in 1999.

So who *did* coin the term? Let's carry on Googling, this time for the pair of phrases "moral panic" "jock young" (capital letters for proper names are not necessary in Google). Now we get 83 unique results on UK web pages. Just going through the list, without even opening any pages, reveals eight references to Jock Young being the originator of the term. The third on the list is a link to the abstract of an article by David G. Bromley in the *Blackwell Encyclopedia of Sociology*. On this link (there's no need to go to the page) we read: 'The term moral panic was initially coined by Jock Young in an essay in Stanley

Cohen's *Images of Deviance* (1971) . . .'. If we Google "David G Bromley" we find straightaway that he is a professor of sociology at Virginia Commonwealth University and has a number of publications to his name, so we might presume that he can be relied on to get things right (although it is careless of him to refer to the book as 'Stanley Cohen's' when Cohen was actually the editor of the book rather than its author).

Not so fast, though. If we do a Google search for the three words "jock young" publications, and open the Wikipedia page at the top of the list,[6] we don't find any reference to a contribution to *Images of Deviance*. We do find him credited with a paper entitled 'The Role of the Police . . .'[7] delivered at a symposium in November 1968. But let's play around a bit. Let's try Googling "jock young" "images of deviance" (pages from the UK only). Aha! Eighth on the list is a web page entitled 'MORAL PANIC: Its Origins in Resistance, Ressentiment and the . . .'. If we click on it we find ourselves at a page[8] with a 'proper' academic paper by Jock Young published in its entirety in the online version of the *British Journal of Criminology* in November 2008. From this paper we learn that his contribution to *Images of Deviance*, edited by Stanley Cohen and published in 1971, was the very paper that he had contributed to the 1968 symposium. Evidently, then, the term 'moral panic' was coined by Jock Young, not Stanley Cohen, and in 1968, not 1971 or 1987. And note that the web has delivered to us a paper so up to date that it would not be on any reading list drawn up when the 2008–09 academic year began.

For the sake of completeness, may I remind you that there is other valuable material on the web besides the more-or-less authoritative writings of academics: law reports, and census and economic data, for example, as well as official documents produced by UK government departments (try Googling "moral panic" "homeoffice.gov.uk"), European Union bodies ("europa.eu") and international bodies such as the United Nations ("un.org"), the World Bank ("worldbank.org") and the International Monetary Fund ("imf.org").

There are a number of lessons that we can draw from this exploration:

- Although a search engine can throw up tens or even hundreds of thousands of references to a term, these can be reduced to a manageable number by introducing more terms and narrowing your search to pages from the UK only and to "ac.uk" sites if necessary.

- No attention should be paid to the order of the results thrown up by a search engine. The fact that a student essay came top of our Google lists underlines the importance of this.

- No search engine is perfect. In this case our Google search for "moral panic" did not reveal Jock Young's paper in the *British Journal of Criminology*.

- Playing around with terms in a search engine can be fruitful – but it can also take up a lot of time.

- It's very easy to get hooked into following up details. It's important to bear in mind that what we are doing at this stage is forming an overview, finding out what materials exist 'out there'. Most detailed, targeted reading should be saved for later, although – as the above exploration shows – in the course of pursuing details new and important materials sometimes emerge.

- Useful material *can* be found on Wikipedia and in orthodox encyclopedias, but *nothing* should be accepted at face value, even if it's written by a professor.

- When searching the web it is crucial to check *every* piece of information we find, even something that is presented as an unassailable fact.

- It's best to go back to original sources whenever possible. As ever, secondary sources should not be relied on unless the original source is unavailable and there is more than one secondary source, they are independent of one another, and they are in agreement.

- The web is a particularly powerful tool when used in conjunction with printed sources: its existence does not allow us (at least in the early twenty-first century) to neglect the printed word. Do not rely on web sources alone!

8

Targeted reading: How to find and use key terms

Your exploratory reading should yield a short list of sections and passages within texts that you've overviewed that look as though you might find them useful when writing your essay. Your job now is to narrow down your selection – to paragraphs rather than chapters, for example – to check that these are relevant to your topic, and then to focus on them and work through them thoroughly. Your reading is now 'targeted'.

To select your target passages, there is a two-stage technique that you can use. The first stage involves identifying key terms (words and expressions); the second involves using those key terms to scan for relevant material. The first section below deals with the first of those; the subsequent section deals with the second.

Identifying key terms

When you set out to identify key terms, your starting point will be the topic for your essay. Irrespective of the way your topic is framed – for example, as a direct question, as a statement which you're expected to discuss, as a task or problem, or as nothing more than a subject to write about – turn your attention to the actual words and expressions in the topic, and make a note of the following:

- those words and expressions that you think have a particular significance in the subject that you're studying

- the *phenomena* (including events and situations), the *themes* or the *issues* that are mentioned in the topic

- the names (of people, places, etc.) that are mentioned

- any systems, structures, relationships (especially cause-and-effect ones) and/or processes that are mentioned or implied

- any categories or classes mentioned

- any theories, propositions, concepts and ideas mentioned

- the names of any writers mentioned

- any specialized terms mentioned if you haven't already included them under another heading. (For example, for a law topic these would include statutes and cases.)

As a safeguard, ask yourself whether there are other key terms that you should also make a note of even though they are not specifically mentioned in the topic. For example, is there a particular writer or a particular concept you need to cover? Look at your lecture handouts, reading lists and any notes that you have, and pick out these extra key terms and add them to your list.

Look, too, at past exam papers to see if there are other key terms that tend to be associated in exam topics with those you've already identified. If there are, add these others. Past exam papers will also give you some insight into how your teachers think about their subject.

You now have a list of key terms. Most of them should be specific enough to be found in the index of a book on the subject. Your list needs to be short and manageable. If it's a long list, look for ways of shortening it. Perhaps it could be divided into a short essential list and an additional list. If some of the terms seem too general, look for more specific ones to replace them with.

Scanning for relevant material

In this section I'm dealing primarily with 'unitary' books, i.e. ones that are written as a whole by one or (sometimes) two authors, but the same approach can be applied to edited books that consist of a collection of chapters by a number of authors, and to articles in journals.

I suggest that you adopt the following procedure. You will need to have by you some sheets of A4 paper and a large stack of Post-its®: 5 in. by 3 in. (13 cm by 8 cm) is the most convenient size, and you might like to have them in a range of colours. The idea is to use them as bookmarks.

Table 5 sets out the seven steps in scanning a book.

Table 5   Seven steps in scanning a book

Step	Task
1	Remind yourself of your key terms
2	Scan the contents page
3	Scan the index
4	More bookmarks
5	Scan the whole book
6	Photocopy the most important bits (optional but recommended)
7	Organize and apply your results

Step 1: Remind yourself of your key terms

Write or type out your list of key terms, in large print, on a piece of paper with nothing else on it. Ideally, use colours or highlighter to make the words stand out. Read the list aloud half a dozen times (quietly if you're in the library), and move a finger down the list each time as you do so. All this is to prime your mind for the search you're about to make.

Step 2: Scan the contents page

Open the book at the contents page (the list of chapters), and look down the page to see if one of your key terms is actually a chapter title, or appears in a chapter title. (This should take you only a few seconds.) If your key term is there, find the start of that chapter and stick a Post-it in there, with the top half or third sticking out above the book, to act as a bookmark. *Do not start reading yet!*

Step 3: Scan the index

Now go to the first page of the index at the back of the book. Run your index (!) finger steadily but quickly down the columns of the index, column by column, and follow your fingertip with your eyes. *Do not read the words that are written there!* If you find yourself reading them, you are either going too slowly, in which case move your finger faster, or you are focusing too hard, in which case relax your eyes and just gaze at the page above your fingertip. If you have primed your mind well, when you get to one of your key terms it will automatically catch your eye. This is exactly what you want to happen! With practice, words and expressions will leap off the page at you.

When one of your key terms catches your eye, take your list of key terms and by that particular one make a note of the page number or numbers (if there's a sequence, for example 102–9, note just the first) and then carry on running your finger down the columns until the next key term catches your eye. Again, note the page number(s) and carry on. You should get to the end of the index no more than three or four minutes after you started.

Step 4: More bookmarks

Find each of the pages that you noted in the index exercise of step 3, and stick a Post-it there. If it's the left-hand page of a two-page spread, stick it on the right-hand one, again with part of the Post-it sticking out of the book.

Step 5: Scan the whole book

Look again at your list of key terms, move your finger down the list and read them out loud again, just to remind yourself of them. Now it's time to scan the whole book. Turn to the first page of text (it may be a preface, or introduction, or chapter 1). You're going to do what you did with the index, but because you're working with a page width instead of a column you might like to use two fingers: the index and the middle fingers. Move those fingers steadily but quite quickly straight down the middle of the page – first the left-hand page of a two-page spread and then the right-hand page – and follow your fingertips with your eyes. This should take you no more than a couple of seconds per page. When you get to the foot of the right-hand page, turn over and carry on scanning.

Again, *don't read the sentences yet!* If you find yourself reading the actual words and trying to make sense of them you're either going too slowly: speed up! or you're focusing too hard: relax! (Incidentally, a sign that your eyes are nicely relaxed is that you can see *two* vertical creases between the left- and right-hand pages: the parallax effect.) And don't worry that you might be missing words at the edges of pages (i.e. the beginnings and ends of lines): your peripheral vision will take care of those.

When one of your key terms catches your eye, grab a Post-it and stick it on the page in the usual fashion. Jot down the page number on the Post-it and a brief note of what's there. When you come to a Post-it that you put in earlier, when doing the index exercise, see if there actually is a key term nearby that you can mark with it.

Get to the end of the book as quickly as you can. Around fifteen minutes for a 250-page book would be about right. (I'm not joking: remember that what you're doing is *scanning*, not reading as such.)

Do this for all the pieces of reading you're going to use. (Different colour Post-its come in handy to denote different books or articles.) If you are in the habit of reading slowly and carefully in order not to miss anything, you will find it very comforting and reassuring to have these bookmarks.

Step 6: Photocopy the most important bits (optional but recommended)

You now have a book that may be bristling with Post-its. If these cluster together, photocopy those pages and any others needed to complete a chapter or section. (Take care to lift Post-its off pages while you're photocopying them.)

Step 7: Organize and apply your results

Your final task in the scanning process is that of organizing your work and applying it to your task.

If you are able to hold on to the book for a little while longer, it would be a good idea at this point to spend some time on appreciating the topic that you have to work on, and creating a first draft of a plan for your essay (see Chapter 18). It will give you a stronger sense of what bits of the book are relevant if you can see how you would use them in your essay.

If the book you've been using is one that you've borrowed and have to return, go through it, starting at the beginning, finding and retrieving your Post-its one by one. At each one you come to, read the passage referring to your key term and ask yourself whether it is relevant to your task and accordingly worth making a note of. You might consider that the passage is merely a passing reference, or duplicates something better expressed elsewhere, in which case simply remove that Post-it and go on to the next.

When you come to a worthwhile reference, make a note of it. If you are making a mini-dictionary or personal user manual for the course, you may want to make some entries in it. Alternatively, make your note on a piece of paper (see below for ideas on making notes) or electronically, or on the Post-it itself. A very brief note will do if the Post-it is on a page that you have photo-copied. Make sure the Post-it also has the page number on it, then remove it. Keep doing this until you have removed all of the Post-its from the book.

An optional but neat thing to do with all those Post-its is this. Get yourself a sheet of flipchart paper and stick the Post-its on to it. Now move them around until related ones are clustered together and, ideally, the clusters themselves are in a logical relationship to one another. Stick the sheet of flipchart paper on your wall with a piece of Blu-Tack® or something similar. You can add further Post-its produced by reading more books or articles, building up your clusters or creating fresh ones, all on the same piece of paper.

When you're happy with the arrangement, you might like to draw lines to connect related clusters.

Doing all this will engage your mind. Sticking up Post-its and moving them around sounds like a simple activity, but it will familiarize you with the material and get you thinking about what clusters with what, and about what relationships and connections you can find. It will also help you to remember what you have been thinking about. If the book you've been using is your own, you might be content to leave the Post-its in place. The important thing is that when you are drafting your essay you know exactly where to find the material you want.

This completes your scan of the book you've been working on. Treat other books in the same way, add the resultant notes and Post-its to your collection, and incorporate them all into your own personal user manual for your course. (See Chapter 9 for advice on creating a user manual for yourself.)

How to scan an article or chapter

You can follow exactly the same approach with a chapter or journal article. These won't have contents lists, so make your own and then go through the same steps as for a unitary book. Again, remember that it will be helpful for you to be in that receptive state of mind where your key terms will jump off the page at you. So once again, follow your fingertips steadily down the pages at a speed fast enough for you not to lapse into actual reading.

9

Dedicated reading:
How to master a text

Dedicated reading is the third of the reading strategies I introduced in Chapter 5. It involves working your way through a text (a book, chapter or article) which you have to master if you are to do well in your exam. Your special goal is to gain an understanding of the material and make it 'yours'. In this third stage in the learning process (after selecting/copying and translating, see Chapter 2), you will come to feel that you 'know' the material. You will be able to use the author's language fluently, to describe concepts accurately in your own words, and to apply them appropriately. You will also find that you are beginning to develop a critical eye and a critical 'voice' of your own.

To attain this goal, it will be extremely helpful to you – indeed, it's really a necessity – to have your own copy of the book or a photocopy of the chapter or article. You should also be prepared to write in the book: if you're unhappy about doing this, try to bring yourself to use a soft (2B) pencil so you can easily erase notes and markings later. Even if you only put sidelines in the margin, this does help you to make the material yours.

Unless you're very much on your own, there should be a good deal of help already available to you when you set out to master a text. Lectures and lecture handouts, class and tutorial discussions should all help. There's more about using these below.

Here are some preliminary things to do with the text:

■ Do an exploratory read using the suggestions in previous chapters.

■ Simply look through the text, from beginning to end, and repeat this regularly. It will become less intimidating as you become more familiar with it: you reach a point where you can open it at any page and recognize immediately the words or diagrams, figures and tables that you see in front of you.

■ If the text is a book that has a full contents list – i.e. not only chapter headings but section headings too – make a photocopy of the list. If it doesn't have a full contents list, go through it and compile your own. On your list, tick off any chapters and sections that you feel you understand and don't have a problem with.

■ Articles in journals and self-contained chapters in edited collections won't have their own list of contents or their own index. If you haven't already done so, make your own contents list by going through the text and listing the headings that you find. When you have done this you will immediately feel much more comfortable with the text.

Now you need to prioritize, to decide what elements in your text or texts are calling for your urgent and immediate attention, so you have to deal with them first. This could be dictated by your teaching programme, or by the need to get certain fundamentals under your belt before you can make progress.

As with targeted reading, you need to get down to essentials. Choose one of your top priority texts and examine it to see if there's anything in it you can ignore for the moment (e.g. fine detail, examples, side issues, commentary, discussion of other writers' work), and on your contents list bracket these bits off in square brackets [   ].

Now actual work can be delayed no longer. Take the first sentence of the first passage in front of you. Do you understand it? If it seems complicated, see if you can break it down into two or more short sentences: the shorter the better. Now paraphrase each sentence: express it differently in your own words, in language you can understand.

This exercise should reveal to you any terms – words or expressions – whose meaning isn't clear to you. It's crucial that you master these. Look back at Box 1 ('Translating academic-speak') on pages 12–14 to remind yourself of the level of detail required for this. Remember that academic-speak is, to all intents and purposes, a foreign language. So make your own mini-dictionary/phrasebook for the subject. When you come across a word, expression, sentence, diagram or whatever that you don't immediately understand, puzzle out its meaning – which means translating it into language that you *do* understand. Look it up in other books, or ask your teacher for help. Then write it down on a sheet of punched paper, so you now have a note of its meaning, and/or examples of how to use the term, for your own use. Put the sheet in a ring binder. You have started your mini-dictionary.

Once you've started your mini-dictionary, keep a lookout for different definitions of the same word. This will tell you that you're in a field where different writers may use the same word to mean different things: that's to say, you're dealing with meanings rather than standard definitions. It's important to be aware of this. You can extend your mini-dictionary by adding sheets on the concepts, theories, other authors etc. that you encounter in the book. Don't forget to note the numbers of the pages where you found them.

You might find it useful to take this idea further and create your own 'user manual' for each of the courses that you are taking, incorporating your mini-dictionary, lecture notes and handouts, worked examples and problems, past exam papers, reading lists and essay topics, and any other material that comes your way.

NB Observe that for some subjects you may need a multiple dictionary. For example, in the case of economics you may need a four-column dictionary: ordinary English; economics-speak; diagrams; equations. Faced with a question in 'ordinary' English, you'll need to translate it into technical language (economics-speak) and then create the necessary diagram or find the appropriate equation to arrive at your answer, which then has to be translated back into economics-speak and again into ordinary English.

Work your way steadily through the significant passages in the text. The first time through, skip – if you can – those that you find really difficult. You can come back to them later, maybe after a lecture or class, or after you've asked someone for help. Sometimes looking at past exam questions will give you a clue as to the significance of a passage. Sometimes going to the end of the text – for example, leapfrogging to discussion or conclusions – will help. Gradually you'll find that the passages you don't understand are reduced to little islands in the text. With the bulk of it under your belt, you can then polish these off one by one.

Cross-check all your material. Remember that you're doing detective work, just as we did in the 'moral panic' exercise in using the web (Chapter 7). Look up in other texts or your lecture notes the words, concepts, theories, authors that you found in your first text and included in your mini-dictionary. Sometimes what you find will confirm what you already knew; often it will extend your knowledge or provoke you to further thoughts, and so enable you to make useful additions to your user manual. Cross-checking like this will broaden your knowledge and deepen your understanding and help the material to stick in your mind. At this stage you are thoroughly engaging with the subject, and you'll find that writing in your own words – rather than simply quoting or paraphrasing the writers you've encountered – is beginning to come easily to you. I promise!

10

How to work with secondary sources

When you're reading an academic text, you'll invariably find that the writer has referred to other texts and has either incorporated original words – quotations, in quotation marks – from them, or has paraphrased the original. The original is known as the primary source; the one you're reading now is the secondary source.

What should you do if the material that's quoted or paraphrased in the secondary source appeals to you, if you'd like to use it yourself in your essay? Ideally, and much to be preferred, you would go and find the original, primary source and consult it for yourself. If that isn't possible, you clearly can't check whether the author of the secondary source has actually quoted or paraphrased accurately. What you can do, though, is to make a basic check of whether its 'status' – its contribution to reasoning – is actually what the author of the secondary source presents it as. For example, you can check whether an opinion in the primary source has been presented as a fact, or if a fact has been presented as an opinion.

You will find, I'm afraid, that many academic writers do not clearly convey the status of quotations and paraphrasings they are using. Writers on plagiarism seem to be particularly prone to this failing. In Table 6 I give some examples where the author of the secondary source clearly (in my judgment, but see what you think) misleads the reader as to the status of the material that he or she has found in the primary source.

Table 6 Misleading citing of quotations and paraphrasings

Quotation/paraphrasing by the author of a secondary source	Comment
Vigue (1997) points out that there has always been the filing cabinet at the fraternity house where students could swap assignments . . . [1]	The term 'points out' suggests that a fact is being adduced. What we have here, however, is an unverifiable historical generalization that the secondary authors are treating as a fact
Connors . . . argues that the Internet has made access to information and to pre-written essays very easy . . . [2]	This isn't an argument: it is a demonstrable fact (unless you want to quibble about the precise meaning of 'very easy')
[Park] states that 'plagiarism is doubtless common and getting more so' . . .[3]	Academic writers, like politicians, use the word 'doubtless' when they don't actually have evidence. Regard it as a synonym for 'I think'. The expression 'common and getting more so' is almost meaningless unless quantified
When stresses rise, students see plagiarism as a reasonable and reasonably risk-free way out of difficulties (Bannister and Ashworth, 1998)[4]	Another generalization: does this apply to *all* students? The secondary author avoids referring to the status of this purported fact by doing no more than referencing the primary source
Hart and Friesner suggest that studies of cheating behaviour in the USA date from the 1940s . . . [5]	Here is another purported fact, not a suggestion in the normal sense of that word. We are offered no evidence that no such studies were carried out prior to the 1940s
Waldmann states that because all mature professions have a well-developed code of ethics, this should be reflected in the education of the future professional.[6]	The secondary authors are endorsing the primary author's slide from an 'is' to an 'ought', from a purported fact (about 'all mature professions') to what 'should' be done in the future. And what constitutes a 'mature' profession (bankers, property developers, estate agents?) is of course a matter of opinion

In all the cases in Table 6, my conclusion is that the authors of the secondary sources have shown a lack of rigour and critical thinking in the matter of drawing on primary sources. I would not rely on such secondary sources for anything at all. I urge you to be similarly circumspect if you encounter other writings of this calibre. Do what you can to track down the original, primary sources.

When you get down to writing an essay, you yourself will in effect become the author of a secondary source. For help with the proper use of quotations, see Chapter 20, 'How to use quotations'.

Part 3
Writing essays

11

Discovering what's wanted from you (1): How to clarify the topic

Before you can start building the results of your reading into an essay, you must have some sense of what your teacher wants from you. The first place to look for this is the topic that you've been given. Topics come in five main forms:

- **The direct question**. A sentence with a question mark (?) at the end.

- **The statement**. A proposition or assertion in quotation marks (' ' or " ") followed by the open-ended instruction 'Discuss' or one of its variants (e.g. 'Discuss critically') or the question 'Do you agree?' A statement may also be incorporated, without the quotation marks, for example in a sentence that begins 'Consider/discuss the view that . . .'.

- **The specific instruction**. You're told to do something, such as 'Describe . . .', 'Explain . . .', 'Analyse . . .', 'Compare and contrast . . .'. The instruction gives you a clearer idea of what's wanted than an open-ended instruction such as 'Discuss', although you may still have to guess what your teacher wants (see below).

- **The problem**. You're expected to apply techniques and reasoning to the data given to arrive at a solution.

- **The subject**. You're merely told 'Write about . . .'.

The direct question

The direct question is the most straightforward kind of topic. If you're asked a question, clearly what's wanted is an answer. What is also wanted, though, is a chain of reasoning that will show the reader how you have got from question to answer. Before you can produce either of those, however, you have to comprehend the question, and this may require you to clarify it: to identify and define the key terms, i.e. the key words and expressions, and any ambiguities and traps.

The statement

As with the direct question, you have to comprehend the statement and identify and define key terms, etc. You also have to appreciate why you are being asked to discuss this particular statement. Does your teacher want you to examine the reasoning in the statement and/or the evidence or any underlying assumptions on which it is based? Or to challenge any opinions or value judgments incorporated in it?

Terms such as 'Discuss' and 'Discuss critically' and 'Consider the view' are very open ended, in the sense that they don't actually tell you what you have to do or what the outcome has to be. Accordingly, what you must do is take your cue from the wording of the statement, what it actually says. You should, by the way, treat 'Discuss' and 'Discuss critically' as synonymous: 'Discuss' on its own does *not* signify that you're invited to discuss a statement uncritically!

What meaning, then, should you attribute to the instruction 'Discuss'? Let's say you are required to write an essay on the following topic:

'Plagiarism is the greatest curse of modern education.' Discuss.

You could approach this topic in a variety of ways. In Table 7 I show nine (!) of them. (You may be able to think of others.)

Notice that your choice of approach will depend, if you want to get top marks, on what your teacher wants from you. So you have to find this out. This requires you to figure out your teacher's 'mindset', a task that I address in Chapter 14.

Notice, too, that sometimes a statement can be reformulated as a direct question: you might find it easier to work with in that form. For example, if you ask 'Is plagiarism the greatest curse of modern education?', that will lead you on immediately to ask yourself 'How can I tell whether it is?', and then you're in business. Questions are usually much more useful than instructions. They focus your mind. A good question is incisive, it's like a sharp knife: it cuts through assumptions and waffle.

Table 7   Approaches to a 'discuss' topic

Approach	Comment
Identify the source of the quotation	If the source is not well known, this could show that you have read widely
Provide a dictionary definition of 'curse' and show how to compare the sizes of curses	Shows that you appreciate the need to define your terms and have picked up the significance of the word 'greatest'
Identify other phenomena or behaviours that have been described as curses, and compare the consequences of these with the consequences of plagiarism	Shows that you can identify and apply a systematic approach to your task
Compare plagiarism today with plagiarism in the past	Shows that you have picked up the significance of the word 'modern'
Show you're familiar with the literature on plagiarism	It will be good to show that you're familiar with the literature
Point out the different definitions of 'plagiarism' used in different institutions	Shows that you are aware of the different definitions of 'plagiarism' and the fact that different ones are used in different institutions
Argue that plagiarism isn't a curse at all	This might not go down well with your teacher
Compare and contrast various ways of countering plagiarism	This is not, strictly speaking, what the topic covers, but it could be what your teacher wants
Imagine you're writing an application for a job policing plagiarism	Again, this is not, strictly speaking, what the topic covers, but could be what your teacher would like to see

The specific instruction

While specific instructions give you a clearer target to aim at than does an open-ended instruction such as 'Discuss', you may still have to guess what your teacher wants. The same instruction can have different meanings, as shown in Table 8.

Table 8 Instructions that keep you guessing

Instruction	Possible meanings
'Describe'	1. List the significant characteristics of the subject (in which case you will have to decide which characteristics to regard as significant ones) 2. Say in addition to no. 1 *why* you consider these characteristics to be significant 3. Say in addition to no. 1 and no. 2 how these characteristics are interconnected, e.g. how, if one is present, others will be
'Analyse'	1. Describe in detail 2. Break down into component parts 3. Show how causes combine to bring about certain effects
'Explain'	1. 'Say clearly what is meant by . . .' 2. 'Tell the story of how X came about' 3. 'Show how causes combine to bring about certain effects' 4. 'State the reasons that someone had for behaving in the way they did'
'Compare and contrast'	1. List similarities and differences 2. Formulate and apply criteria that can be used for comparison 3. Say in addition to no. 1 and/or no. 2 how the similarities and differences come about

Beware anyone who tells you that the instructions in the table have only one meaning. It's not so.

The problem

Problem topics are usually fairly straightforward in that they provide you with a certain amount of information – which will be helpful, so long as you know what to do with it. There are certain rules to abide by. For example, don't ignore any piece of information. And if the problem admits of more than one answer, say so, rather than just plumping for one.

Occasionally, however, you may be set a problem topic that is (deliberately or through carelessness on the setter's part) confusing. If you're studying law, you may be accustomed to dividing topics into two kinds: 'discuss' topics – e.g. 'Family law has not kept up with recent demographic change.' Discuss – and problem topics, where a set of circumstances is described and you are then instructed: 'Advise Mary' (or whoever). But you may encounter a 'rogue' topic, in which a set of circumstances is described and you are then instructed 'Discuss the remedies available to Mary'. This is clearly a problem topic, so as usual you have to set out the advice you would give, but there is a twist: you are evidently expected to place your advice in context. That is to say, in addition to giving advice you should show how, for example, it reflects an anomaly in the law or is the result of recent changes in the law.

The subject

If you're merely given a subject as the topic for your essay it won't be apparent when you first look at it what (if anything) you are expected to do. So, as with a direct question or statement, you will have to clarify it and identify the key terms. It's also worth looking at past exam papers for questions on that subject: they may highlight significant aspects of the subject and give you some guidance as to what to focus on.

You could of course ask your teacher for a 'proper' topic: ideally a direct question or a statement to discuss. If you encounter some reluctance, you might meet with more success if you formulate one or two or three topics yourself, and then politely ask whether one of them would be suitable.

Some words of warning are called for here. As a student, you may take it for granted that when your teachers ask you for something they know what they want. Beware: this is not always the case. Some enlightened ones do have an open mind: they set a topic to stimulate and provoke you, to see what you come up with. But others, sadly, are lazy or confused or both.

We see this with topics that contain more than one instruction. For example, you may get a topic that consists of a direct question (ending with a question mark) followed by 'Discuss': anyone with half a brain knows that what a direct question calls for is an answer, not a discussion. You could perhaps respond literally by, for example, discussing whether the question is a good one, but it is unlikely that this is what your teacher wants you to do. (It's not impossible, though, and it would be sensible to check.) I suspect that the teacher who sets a topic consisting of a direct question followed by 'Discuss' is simply confused.

Confusion on the part of academics is also apparent in their tendency to use the same instruction to mean different things (see the examples given in Table 8) and in the habit that many have of asking you a direct question and then telling you that they want to see an argument. Asking you a direct question sets your mind working 'forwards' in 'Q to A' mode, from question to answer, a perfectly logical way of working. But telling you to produce an argument puts you in advocacy mode: it implicitly suggests to you that you should start with your answer, which is certainly not logical. And you can't be both logical and illogical at the same time. If you try to do so, you will scramble your brain: it's a sure-fire recipe for writer's block. I have met many students who have started writing an essay to answer a question with the words 'In this essay I shall argue . . .' and then found themselves completely at a loss as to how to continue. It's as though you're being asked to tell a joke starting with the punchline: what on earth do you say next? You are put in a position where you are scrabbling around for evidence to back up your argument: this is likely to lead you to overlook evidence that does *not* back it up.

If you are asked to 'produce an argument', what should you do? First and foremost, bear in mind that an argument is essentially a logical sequence of steps, a 'chain of reasoning'. In constructing an argument, you are going through a process of assembling your chain of reasoning. But that's just the process: a process is nothing without material to 'feed in' to it, 'ingredients' that contribute to your argument. Those ingredients come in publications of the various types that I listed in Table 4 on page 25. From these publications you extract relevant quotations, within which are found – like pearls inside oysters – ingredients such as facts, perceptions, assumptions, hypotheses, opinions and value judgments. (For a full list see Table 11 on pages 101–3.) These range from objective to subjective, from facts that are common knowledge at the objective end to personal opinions at the subjective end. If you can produce a chain of reasoning that arrives at a conclusion while taking care to distinguish the degree of objectivity/subjectivity of each of the ingredients you've used, your teacher will almost certainly be well pleased.

Sadly, I have never met a student who has been told by a teacher: 'This is how we construct an argument in this discipline', let alone 'This is how to argue!' Likewise, I have never met a student who has been told by a teacher: 'This is how to discuss.' *If you have a teacher who wants you to 'argue' or 'discuss', ask him or her how to do it.* Ask to be shown how. Ask where you can find examples. And try to spend some time in lectures simply observing how they themselves do it: notice what counts as argument or discussion for them, and what makes an argument or discussion a good or sound one. (Get one of

your friends to take notes during those lectures, and then trade your observations for their notes.) Read and inspect closely anything that they themselves have published.

12

Discovering what's wanted from you (2): Traps to avoid

While some essay topics are nice and straightforward, and it's clear what's wanted from you, others are not. Many contain traps for the unwary. If you want to produce a good essay it is absolutely crucial that you are aware of these traps, so you can avoid them. Here are some questions to help you develop this awareness.

- Is it clear to you what the question or statement means, or what the task requires you to do?

If the question or whatever is ambiguous, i.e. it could be interpreted in more than one way, you will need to consider the alternatives and justify your choice in the Introduction to your essay. *Never* jump without thinking to any conclusion about what is expected of you.

- Are there words or expressions in the topic that are capable of more than one meaning, or are colloquial, or figures of speech (especially metaphors), and accordingly need to be interpreted?

If you encounter this situation ask your teacher for help. If English is not your first language, consult a native English speaker too. Again, the Introduction to your essay would be the appropriate place to discuss how these words or expressions should be interpreted, what meanings should be attached to them. Sometimes you can gain clarity by asking the question: 'How would I recognize X if I saw it?'

- Does the topic include what appears to be a statement of fact (e.g. 'In 1990 there was a change . . .')?

If so, ask yourself whether this purported fact is accurate? (Was there indeed such a change in 1990?) In your essay you may want to consider what evidence there is that can be used to support or contradict purported facts, and whether some relevant facts have been omitted.

- Are any assumptions implied or stated explicitly in the topic?

You should identify any assumptions that you find and consider and comment on their validity. Can they be tested against evidence?

■ Does the topic incorporate reasoning: about cause-and-effect relation-ships, for example, as in statements of the type 'A led to B'?

If so, consider whether this reasoning too can be tested against evidence.

■ Does the topic incorporate any generalized terms or generalizations?

If it incorporates a reference to 'people', say, or 'Europe', you will almost always be expected to break these down: to distinguish between men, women and children in the former case, different countries or groups of countries in the latter. With a generalization of any kind, ask yourself: 'Is this statement always valid? Under what circumstances or conditions is it valid/not valid?'

■ Is there a 'hidden' second question or proposition?

With a topic like 'B is the consequence of A: Discuss' be aware of the implied 'hidden' question: 'Is B the consequence of other factors, or of the conjunc-tion of A and other factors?' Be prepared to discuss that possibility. Hardly any phenomena have a single cause.

■ Is your instinctive reaction to agree or disagree with the statement or to answer yes or no to the question?

If so, try to make your thinking explicit, and consider whether there might be certain circumstances under which you would come to a different conclusion.

■ Does the topic include the words 'function' or 'role' or other words which could similarly be used in either a descriptive sense ('X performs the function of . . .') or a normative sense ('X ought to . . .')?

If the question or proposition does not make it clear which sense is intended, you should point out and discuss the ambiguity in your Introduction. Use of these words in the normative sense also invites you to discuss the matter of who is setting the norms.

■ Are any value judgments (crudely, judgments about whether something is good or bad) incorporated in the question or proposition?

Consider whether the question or statement hinges on such value judgments, and whether people with different perspectives or interests would disagree over it.

- Are you yourself being asked to make a value judgment, e.g. to say whether X was a success or a failure?

If so, be sure to make clear the criteria you are using: in this case, the criteria by which you are judging success or failure. It may be that X was a success from one point of view (or one group's point of view) and a failure from another. Note that you are being asked not merely to describe the consequences of X: you are being asked to exercise your judgment.

- Is some kind of context – social, political, economic etc. – mentioned in the question or proposition?

You will usually gain marks for showing that you are aware of the broader context within which it arises. Accordingly you should say whether – in your judgment – it relates to a very special set of circumstances, for example, or to a current contentious issue. Similarly you might point out any wider implications or significance that your answer might have.

- Do any dates, time spans or other time-related words appear in the topic, such as 'today', 'currently', 'always', 'sometimes', 'frequently', 'often', 'rarely', 'recently', 'never'.

These will focus or qualify your answer, and it is crucial that you pay attention to them.

- Are any specialized terms mentioned that you haven't already identified?

Don't overlook these.

- Do the words 'can', 'could', 'may', 'might' appear in the topic?

Be aware that these denote potential – possibility – rather than fact and actuality. You're being asked to consider counterfactuals (alternative 'scenarios'), e.g. what might have happened rather than what actually did.

Box 2 Adding value to 'basic' essays

'Basic' essays are mostly to do with 'stuff' that you need to know before you can get anywhere in this subject: factual material such as names and attributes that you can look up. The topics are ones that you're likely to be asked to write on at the beginning of a course, to introduce you to the subject and help you get a grounding in it. If you encounter such topics towards the end of a course or in an exam, they are likely to form the first part of a two- (or more) part topic.

Some basic essays are definitional or descriptive. The topics open with instructions or questions like 'Define . . .', 'What is . . .?', 'What is meant by/do you understand by . . .?', 'Describe . . .', 'State the principles . . .'. Of course, you can always supply what's wanted in a straightforward, matter-of-fact way. But to add value to your essay, see if you can find more than one definition or description, and comment on any discrepancies you find. This will show your teacher that you have thought about what you were doing, not just looked things up mechanically.

With a topic that opens 'What are the main features of . . .?', you could just list those features. But to add value, say *why* these features are thought to be 'main' – or major or important or significant – and what distinguishes them from lesser features.

With a 'Compare and contrast . . .' topic, again there's a simple thing you could do: just list similarities and differences. To add value in this case, identify and think about the criteria you're using. To give an extremely simple example, if you were comparing butterflies and moths you could write down as a difference that butterflies are active during daylight whereas moths are active at night. Here the criterion is the level of activity at different levels of natural light.

If you are instructed to 'Outline the method used to . . .' or 'Give an account of . . .', it will almost certainly benefit you to be as systematic as you can. If the method involves a sequence of steps, make a list of them. If you are giving an historical account, stick to chronological order and/or append a chronology, a list of significant events with dates. Having a chronology is a particularly good idea if your account 'doubles back' in time, e.g. 'The king had already, ten years before, . . .'.

13

Essay types

There are several different types of essay. I list my version of these types in Table 9. Not surprisingly, the list is very similar to the list of types of publication in Table 4 on page 25. Table 9 also gives samples of the instructions that you may come across for each type in essay topics set for you. There are two things to notice. One is that essays of all types beyond the basic can be 'triggered' by direct questions, statements to be discussed, specific instructions and problems. This opens up the possibility that you can reformulate one kind of trigger as another: for example, you can reformulate a statement as a question, or a question as a problem, or a specific instruction as question or a problem.

Table 9 Essay types and sample instructions

Type	Sample instructions
Basic	(a) Describe . . . (b) What is . . .? (c) What is meant by/do you understand by . . .? (d) Define . . . (e) State the principles . . . (f) What are the key/main/salient features of . . .? (g) Compare and contrast . . . (h) Outline the method used to . . . (i) Give an account of . . .
'Q to A' (Question to Answer)	(a) Why did [a particular event or situation] come about/fail to come about? (b) Why does . . .? (c) Account for . . ./Explain why . . . (d) To what extent [did certain factors play a part in] . . .? (e) 'X was responsible for . . .' Discuss. (f) What are the causes of . . . (g) What mechanism gives rise to . . .?

Report on an investigation	(a) Describe an experiment you would carry out to . . . (b) Give an account of an experiment you have carried out to . . . Comment on the reliability/significance of your findings. (c) How would you test the hypothesis that . . .?
Review	(a) How comparable are . . .? (b) How can we reconcile . . .? (c) In what ways . . .? (d) 'There is widespread agreement/no agreement as to . . .' Discuss/Do you agree?
Theory	(a) How does X's theory/concept of . . . help us to understand . . .? (b) Critically evaluate X's theory of . . . (c) How applicable is . . . to . . .? (d) [Quotation] Discuss/Comment/Do you agree? (e) Comment on the view that . . . (f) Discuss/Explore/Comment on the assumptions underlying . . .
Argument/ critique of argument	(a) How well founded is the argument that . . .? (b) What argument/case can be made for . . .? (c) [Quotation/statement] Discuss/Comment/Do you agree? (d) Comment on/Critically evaluate the claim that . . .
Issue-centred/ advocacy	(a) What problems face . . .? (b) Comment on/how would you evaluate proposals to . . . (c) How should . . .? (d) 'X can never succeed [unless] . . .' Discuss/Do you agree? (e) Under what conditions can . . .? (f) Write a report advising . . .
Theme-based	Any of the instructions listed above

Academics tend to like their students to produce essays of particular types. Which types they like best will depend on their own 'mindsets'. I deal with teachers' mindsets in the next chapter.

14

How to figure out your teachers' mindsets

Every academic brings to his or her teaching a 'mindset': a collection of preconceptions and taken-for-granteds that they aren't consciously aware of but which are manifest in everything they say and write. Almost certainly what your teacher wants from you is an essay that is consistent with this mindset. If you can take on your teacher's mindset when writing an essay, what you're doing is – in effect – writing for them in a language they can understand: this cannot but help you to get a good grade. So an important part of finding out what your teacher really wants is figuring out his or her mindset.

Figuring out someone else's mindset isn't as difficult as it sounds once you realize what you have to do. And because it involves detective work, doing it can be quite fun. It requires you to pay close attention to your teachers' styles and the very language they use, especially in their lectures and their writings, as well as in the essay topics and exam questions they set. In Table 10 I list the academic mindsets that tend to be associated with particular essay types and offer some suggestions as to what to look for to identify them. Look and listen carefully, and do check out your impressions with your fellow students.

Table 10 Essay types and associated mindsets

Type	Features of associated mindsets
Basic	Stresses basic stuff that you need to know: factual material, things you can look up. Lectures start from first principles, courses build step by step. They tend to be well organized: your essays should be too.
'Q to A' (Question to Answer)	Lectures and writings open with questions chosen because they are puzzles that have attracted the teacher's interest. They may be of different kinds: not just 'Why did X happen?' but 'Why did it happen when it did/where it did/in the form that it did?' Notice if they supplement these with counterfactual questions: 'rather than at some other time/at some other place/in some other form?' Notice too how answers to questions are arrived at, e.g. by citing prior

	events/situations (hence a good deal of narrative), or the conjunction of certain factors, or the writings of other academics: you should follow the same pattern in your essays. Notice what counts as a good answer: one that is 'plausible' or 'well argued', perhaps? Notice if a 'good' answer is one that carries authority: 'To me, the weight of evidence clearly supports X's argument.' The crucial words here are 'to me': look out for hints that you contradict at your peril. Are lectures and writings aimed at explanation, at uncovering mechanisms and processes? Is consistency with observations (evidence) and theories the aim, rather than mere plausibility? If so, your approach must have these aims too.
Report on an investigation	Notice whether this takes the form of a straightforward, 'linear' progression from the objective of the investigation (could be to test an hypothesis, or to see what happens when . . .) through theoretical background, methodology, observations (data collected), findings (analysis of data collected), interpretation/significance of findings (results), to conclusions. Or does the author omit steps or take them out of their logical sequence? Notice also the steps during which choices are made and judgment exercised, and how self-critical or self-justificatory the presentation is.
Review	Notice whether this is done in a very compartmentalized and/or uncritical way ('X says . . .', 'According to Y, . . .', 'Let me now turn to Z, . . .'). Alternatively, are connections made: contributions put together, similarities and differences highlighted, syntheses made, conclusions drawn? Try to be as systematic as you can.
Theory	Notice how high the level of academic-speak is, and how much name dropping. Some academics teach as if the literature on the subject were itself the subject. Look out for courses on 'great thinkers' and examination papers consisting largely or entirely of quotations from their works which you are instructed to 'discuss' or 'discuss critically'. You will need to draw heavily on the literature yourself. Notice whether any 'raw' data drawn from the 'real world' is cited. (If not, never ever introduce such material in your essays, especially anything drawn from your personal life experience.)
Argument/ critique of argument	Some teachers see their task as one of persuasion. Listen for their use of the words 'argue' and 'argument' – 'In this lecture I shall argue that . . .', 'My argument is . . .' – and lectures that are essentially attempts to persuade you that their point of view is correct. Notice how they construct their arguments and what kind of material they cite in support of them. Notice too how they deal with material that does not support them (do they ignore it?) and how

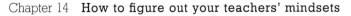

	they treat authors with whom they disagree. If their approach seems sloppy to you, try to do better, but use their language when you can.
Issue-centred/ advocacy	Notice the procedure for getting from the issue – the 'what should be done?' question – to the proposal, usually via formulating alternative courses of action, assessing their actual/likely consequences, and then applying value judgments. Notice where the words 'must', 'ought' and 'should' start appearing. Again, if your teachers' approach seems sloppy to you, try to do better, but use their language when you can.
Theme-based	Listen for definitions of abstract terms such as 'theme', 'aspect' and 'perspective', and try to make explicit the meaning or meanings given to each one. They are liable to be all-encompassing and general, rather than enabling you to recognize an X when you see it, but you need to be aware if this is the case. Try to break down the presentation into component parts. Do these form a logical progression? If not, do they amount to a 'collage', a patchwork of facts, research findings, quotations, critiques, categorizations, opinions, appeals to common sense, etc.? And notice the use of metaphor, for example in titles like 'Molehills into mountains: a study of the growth of universities'. Yet again, if the approach seems sloppy to you, try to do better, but use their language when you can. In particular, keep your eyes and ears open for clues about the 'methodology' being employed. If teachers start a lecture by saying they are going to explore, discuss or consider something, do notice *how* they go about exploring, discussing or considering. You will need to follow their example in your own essays and presentations, but it is very unlikely that they will consciously set out to teach you how it's done.

Note that few academics take exactly the same approach to teaching a subject as their colleagues do. So compare the approaches of different teachers, both within and across disciplines. Compare the ways in which they structure lectures, their preferences as to exam questions, how they use published materials.

I must stress that these mindsets apply to *teaching*. Interestingly, academics seem to operate with very different mindsets when they're doing their own *research*. There are quite extraordinary discrepancies here. For example:

■ An historian enquiring into the causes of an event or development works backwards in time. But the results are delivered to students as a narrative going forwards in time.

■ Law students find themselves being taught 'the law' rather than how to reason as a lawyer.

■ Economists present their subject to students as an analytical one, making use of graphs and equations, but their debates among themselves reveal economics to be a subject rooted in argument, not pure analysis. (Your suspicions might be aroused by the fact that the material presented to students by the authors of elementary economics textbooks is often not 'real' data drawn from statistics on economic activity but fictitious data on the supply and consumption of butter, or fictitious scenarios: 'Imagine you are running a squash club . . .'. To a scientist, the idea of presenting fiction in a textbook is preposterous.)

■ A student opening a standard text on government or public/social policy will find a definition of 'policy' which is so general and abstract as to be quite useless for investigative purposes because it doesn't enable you to recognize a policy when you see it. Researchers in this field don't actually make use of such definitions.

■ A physicist doing research starts with puzzling observations and asks, 'Why is this the way it is?', but succeeding generations of students then carry out experiments not to address the puzzle but to demonstrate the validity of the law or theory formulated to explain it.

■ The chemistry teacher who, in my hearing at a conference, described his subject as a 'factual' one clearly has no notion of teaching his students how chemists think when they're doing research.

I don't claim that the above generalizations apply to every teacher and every course. But there does seem to be a common pattern of academics using very different mindsets in their textbook-based undergraduate teaching on the one hand and in their research and professional discussion and debate on the other.

What are the implications for you, as a student? In Chapter 2 I suggested that in order to do well you need to learn not only subject matter but also how your teachers think. What I'm saying now is that your teachers think in more than one way – with their teaching mindset and with their research mindset – and you need to acquire both ways of thinking. So, once you get beyond the early stages of your course, don't limit yourself to textbooks. Read the professional literature, to familiarize yourself with how researchers in your field see the world. And do a bit of comparing and contrasting. Ask yourself questions such as, 'Do economists think differently from economic histor-ians?', and then try to put your finger on the differences that you observe.

15

How your essay will be marked (1): 'Tick-box' marking

One of your tasks as a student is to carry out your own little research projects to discover how your essays will be marked. Please don't make any assumptions about this. You need to *know* what you will gain and lose marks for. Knowing this is one of the secrets of doing well in higher education.

In my experience, there are – broadly speaking – two kinds of marking: 'tick-box' marking and impressionistic marking. Tick-box marking is done by seeing whether your essay meets certain objective criteria. For example, have you understood the question? Have you read and used all the essential reading? Have you correctly referenced all the sources you've used? If you've done all these, the marker can tick the corresponding boxes, and you will be given marks for your efforts. If you haven't done these, then the boxes go unticked, and you don't get the marks.

The first rule is that you must listen to what your teachers tell you. So if your teacher tells you 'I'm not interested in what you think, I'm interested in what you've read', as might happen early in a course, you really must restrain your personal opinions, avoid using the words 'I think', and concentrate on showing that you have grasped what's in the literature. Do not – absolutely not! – go off on a frolic of your own.

The second rule is that you must do your best to get useful feedback. Ask for it if you don't get it. Always ask how you could have done better, even if you get a top mark. If you're in your final year, ask what would need to be added to or changed in your essay to make it really good. Try to get as much detail in feedback as you can: this is the most reliable guide to the criteria that the marker is applying.

The third rule is that you should consult and make use of your department's marking scheme. Across UK universities there are hundreds of these, and consequently a huge variety. (Try doing Google searches for "marking scheme" and "mark scheme"!)

By far the most common form of marking scheme consists of a table with a number of columns. Typically one column is headed 'Class', another is headed

'Mark Range' or 'Numerical Range', while in a third are listed the criteria appropriate to each class and mark range.

Many marking schemes are couched in very uninformative language. For example, in the generic marking scheme in use at Exeter University in 2008–09, you will find that the criteria corresponding to the mark range 50–59 per cent (Competent, Class 2:2) are: 'Competent, largely descriptive in approach, generally sound, adequate or routine knowledge of subject, generally satisfactory'.[1]

Imagine you are an Exeter student who has written an essay and received it back with a mark of 45 per cent. The marking scheme tells you that it is 'weak, Third Class': 'Some evidence of learning outcomes having been achieved, but muddled, poorly argued, inadequate deployment of critical method, lacking focus, lacking depth of understanding, some important elements missing, a significant error, seriously deficient analytical skills.' To discover all this will both discourage you and not tell you very much. So, even if you have been given some marginal and overall comments that will help, go and see your teacher, taking your essay with you, and ask him or her to point out exactly which of these defects apply to your essay – exactly *where* it is muddled, lacking focus, lacking depth of understanding, etc. – and how to improve it. You could also ask to be shown which 'learning outcomes' you have failed to achieve. (Of course, you could also set your sights on raising your game and getting into the 2:2 bracket, and ask what would make your essay 'generally sound and satisfactory', but this may not be terribly productive as a way of eliciting a useful response.)

There is another, less common, form of marking scheme that literally offers markers a selection of boxes to tick. The Universities of both Kent and Leeds have (almost) the identical page, headed 'Essay Marking Criteria', on their websites[2] but on neither page do we find anyone credited as the originator. On this page we find a column with a list of thirteen criteria, grouped under four headings: Knowledge, Essay, Personal, and Critical Theory. By each criterion there are five boxes, representing a scale: the marker can tick the box that corresponds most closely to the standard achieved by the essay. For example, under 'Knowledge' we find the criterion 'Genre', with a range from 'Wide knowledge used in analysis' to 'No knowledge or not used'. Under 'Essay' we find the criterion 'Structure', with a range from 'Clear, logical structure' to 'Confused list'. Under 'Personal' we find 'Response to text', with a range from 'Vivid, personal' to 'Little response'. And under 'Critical Theory' we find 'Understanding', with a range from 'Clear grasp' to 'Little grasp'.

By exploring the Kent web address a little we find that in fact the author of this marking scheme is Dr Chris Rust, of Oxford Brookes University. In November 2007 he presented it at a seminar at the University of Kent.[3] His scheme has three merits. One is that students can use it to perform a self-assessment: when this is compared with the marker's assessment differences between the two are readily apparent, and feedback can concentrate on these. Another is of course that exactly the same criteria are applied across the whole range from First Class to Fail. And the third is that it avoids the use of grossly unhelpful terms such as 'Very good' and 'Generally satisfactory'. If you find that the feedback you are getting from your teachers is not constructive, why not download Chris Rust's essay-marking criteria for yourself and ask your teachers to use it to pinpoint where you could improve?

16

How your essay will be marked (2): Impressionistic marking

As the great variety of marking schemes and the accepted need for double-marking of assessed work and exam scripts demonstrates, essay marking is not an exact science. Some scope for subjectivity is unavoidable. For example, if your course is one that 'builds' through the year (rather than being divided into self-contained chunks), the marker has a choice: he or she can mark your first few essays in a way that recognizes you are new to the subject, or mark it as if it had been written at the end of the year, applying examination-level standards. A mark awarded on the former basis might give you a false sense of your level and the standards expected overall, and if it led you to rely on the essay for revision for your exam you might do rather poorly, while a mark awarded on the latter basis might leave you very discouraged. Find out as much as you can about what individual teachers do.

The scope for subjectivity allows academics to give your essay a mark based on their impression of it, an irresistible temptation if they have a huge stack of essays to get through in a limited time. Here are some of the indicators – 'clues' – that will give them a poor impression:

- Prefacing your essay with a quotation that is not relevant to the topic set. This is sure to have set you off on the wrong track.

- Arbitrarily narrowing the topic: for example, saying you will discuss only certain aspects without giving any justification for doing so. This shows you are avoiding considering the full implications of the question.

- Not providing an introduction but jumping straight into your discussion. This suggests that you haven't given much thought to how to approach the topic and organize your essay.

- Not providing any analysis or interpretation of the topic. This suggests you haven't bothered to question anything in the topic.

- If the topic is a question, not answering it. Evading a question is a guaranteed mark loser.

- Using only textbooks as your sources. This marks your essay as a 2:2 or Third straight away.

- Writing everything you know about the subject. This shows you haven't distinguished between what's relevant and what isn't.

- Writing like a textbook. This gives the impression that you are pretending to have authority that, as a student, you don't have. It will also bore the marker.

- Simply regurgitating what your teacher has told you, adding nothing of your own. This suggests that your approach is uncritical, and that you have not thought about what you have been told. This too will bore the marker.

- Writing sloppily, using colloquial language, and being illogical, e.g. saying 'Before answering the question it is necessary to . . .' without saying why it is necessary. Sloppy language and lack of logic both indicate a lack of academic quality.

- Writing in a disjointed way, so that one paragraph does not follow on logically from the next. This results in your essay not having a clear structure, which shows that you don't have a systematic approach, and suggests that you have not thought clearly about the topic.

- Not citing your sources or, if you do cite them, not referencing them fully and consistently. This demonstrates carelessness on your part, as well as a disregard for academic conventions.

If you avoid all the above, your essay is more likely to be read carefully, and you are more likely to get useful comments on it.

What are the clues that alerts the marker to the possibility that he or she is reading something really good? This is more difficult to be categorical about, but there are some valuable insights to be gained from an experiment that was carried out in 1996 by the History Faculty Board at Cambridge. Concerned that women were under-represented among those gaining First Class Honours, the Board enterprisingly set their students a mock finals examination and then held a mock examiners' meeting on it. As a mock meeting it was not subject to the normal confidentiality restrictions, and indeed it was video-recorded and extracts from the recording were broadcast on BBC2 in November 1996.[1]

One of the questions set for the mock exam was on wars. A televised extract from the mock examiners' meeting revealed some of the criteria being used for assessment:

[The] range of wars discussed was terribly impressive . . . all sorts of wars I'd never heard of were here.

I liked some of the allusions to the literature . . . [such an allusion] always spices up an essay.

Bringing up the trade wars was I thought a very neat idea.

There was no mention of theories about war, and that might well be a significant failing.

On this evidence, successful students hadn't merely mastered the subject matter and remembered to bring in theories where appropriate: they found ways of impressing and surprising the examiners – with the lateral thinking they had brought to their reading, their imaginative interpretation of the question, and their skilful deployment of spicy allusions. (It also appeared that male students were more likely to do this by virtue of being more adventurous in their approach, forcefully pursuing an argument rather than presenting a balanced consideration of a range of points of view, and venturing further in their reading.) These aren't criteria to be found in conventional marking schemes.

To a considerable extent, then, what the successful students had done was to get themselves taken seriously by their teachers. They had acquired something of the professional mindset of their teachers, and the expertise that goes with it, so their writings were treated as worth paying attention to. They had learned to be and to think like historians, and were being assessed on that basis. Moreover, the skills they had learned to deploy – lateral thinking, using their imagination, making neat allusions – were clearly not ones they had been consciously taught, or their examiners would not have been surprised and impressed.

The lesson here? I think it's that if you get to know your subject well, and can then free your mind from the mental straightjacket that immersion in other people's writings is liable to induce, you can do very well indeed.

Get useful feedback

On the face of it, feedback, in the form of marks and comments on essays, should be an accurate way of discovering what criteria are being used in practice in marking your essays. Unfortunately, it is a common complaint among students that they don't get useful feedback on their essays. Sometimes the complaint is that marks aren't given, so they don't know how they are doing; sometimes it's that comments are very sketchy or that they are all criticism, and don't help the student to do better next time.

Rather than press your teacher for a mark, I suggest you ask the four crucial feedback questions:

- What did I do well?

- What did I not do well?

- How could I have improved the essay?

- How can I do better next time?

Considered answers to these questions will help you to see what progress you are making, and will be of far more value to you than a mark.

17

Thinking it through: the importance of methodology

Once you have clarified the topic on which you're going to write, you'll see that if it calls for more than a basic essay you will have to think quite hard about how you are going to go about it: what methodology you will use and what materials you will need.

The notion of methodology is an important one to grasp. Your methodology is simply your way of working, your 'system of methods'. You can't *not* have a methodology: that is to say, you will assuredly have one even if you are unaware of it. For example, take the direct question: Why did Bismarck resign his position as Chancellor of the German empire in 1890? Here are four possible methodologies for answering it.

One: you might consult every historian of that era that you can find, so you end up writing an essay about historians' opinions on the subject.

Two: you could simply narrate (describe) events 'leading up to' his resignation. This of course necessitates some judgment on your part as to which prior events were significant and which were not. So you have to ask yourself: 'How can I tell which prior events were significant and which were not?'

Three: you could construct alternative – counterfactual – scenarios. For example, you could ask yourself whether, if Kaiser Wilhelm II had had a different personality, it is likely that events would have followed the same course.

Four: you could try to put yourself in Bismarck's position just before he resigned, and ask yourself what alternatives were open to him and how he would have felt about them, so in effect you're trying to reconstruct his rationale.

Note that each of these four approaches involves devising and using a methodology. If you aren't clear what methodology you are using, you run the risk of trying to use two, three or even all four at once, which will thoroughly confuse you. You'll end up submitting an unsatisfactory piece of work – if, indeed, you do succeed in completing it!

So what should you do to establish your methodology?

If your topic is in the form of a direct question, ask yourself a further question: '*How can I tell?*' In the above example, you would ask yourself: 'How can I tell why Bismarck resigned?' Ask yourself what information is available on the subject, and what you could do with it. Once you *are* clear about how you are going to work towards finding an answer you might indeed find yourself using more than one methodology: using two or more in combination – consciously! – can be very powerful.

If you are instructed to explain a phenomenon – such as an event, a situation, or an experimental result – again you must think about *how* to do this. What is the connection between the phenomenon and the conditions that existed immediately prior to it? How can you discover the mechanisms that were at work? You must have a methodology for doing any of these.

If you are required to make a comparative study of writings in a field, you will need first to think about and decide on the criteria you are going to use for your comparison. For example, you might want to make a comprehensive examination of each writer's background, perspective, set of assumptions, objectives, language, and contribution to the advancement of the subject. You might want to identify areas of agreement or disagreement, to try to find out how two or more writers or schools of thought come to different conclusions, and to form your own judgment as to which is to be preferred.

If you are required to discuss or comment on a quotation, again you need to have a systematic approach. You might want to do one or more of the following:

- Comment on where the writer is 'coming from'

- Explore the use that he or she makes of certain imagery or literary techniques

- Place the writer in a certain historical, social and/or political context

- Consider which school of thought he or she belongs to

- 'Read between the lines' to see what assumptions or premises the quotation is based on

- Scrutinize the manifest or implied reasoning to search for detect errors or omissions

- Examine the basis of the quotation, asking whether – for example – it is based on accepted knowledge, empirical observation, theory, or an appeal to common sense, and what part value judgments play in it, and so on.

Take particular care when you are writing for teachers whose style is theme-based. They are very prone to use colloquial language. For example, you may be asked to discuss a statement to the effect that such-and-such is 'beyond the pale', or asked the question: 'Does it matter that . . .?'. 'Beyond the pale' and 'Does it matter?' are colloquial expressions, not technical ones, or ones that you will find defined in academic literature. Consequently you will have to ask 'How can I tell whether it was beyond the pale?' or 'How can I tell whether it matters?' when you encounter such language. If your teachers use colloquial language and you follow their example, your writing is liable to lack structure and precision. This is an instance where it is *not* helpful to follow your teachers' example.

18

How to create an essay plan

In order to write a decent essay you need to have a plan. Some exceptional people can manage with a plan that they keep in their heads, but ordinary mortals need to have it written down, on paper or on screen. A plan, which you rough out at the beginning and refine as you go along, provides you with a structure for your essay. Look at marking schemes: almost certainly one of the criteria against which your work will be judged is whether it has a clear and logical structure.

An essay plan is basically a list of headings: main headings and sub-headings. Some teachers don't like to see headings and sub-headings in an essay, and will deduct marks for including them, but that needn't stop you using them when writing: you simply delete them when your essay is finished, before handing it in.

Here are some suggestions for creating your essay plan. They will be suitable for essays of all the types listed in Table 9. All of these suggestions are to do with marshalling relevant materials – 'raw' materials, writings, whatever – giving them your personal treatment, and coming to reasoned conclusions. As I see it, that is what scholarship is all about and that is the business we are all in, teachers and students, in all academic subjects.

To begin, make a list of main headings for yourself. Your initial list might look like this:

- **Introduction** (Every essay needs an introduction!)

- **Methodology** (If you're going to use a specific method or approach, you might prefer to give this section the name of that method or approach, e.g. 'Content Analysis' or 'The Feminist Perspective'.)

- **Materials Used** (You might want to give this section a more descriptive name, e.g. 'The Case Studies' or 'The Literature'.)

- **Analysis** (This is where you describe your reasoning – how you applied your methodology to your materials – and the results or findings that emerged. You might want to give this section a heading that relates to your specific subject, rather than the generic heading of 'Analysis'.)

- **Discussion**

- **Conclusions** (or Conclusion).

This is a very bare skeleton of a list, but it does give you the beginnings of a plan for your essay. Now put some flesh on the skeleton, by working your way down the list, jotting down your ideas about what should go under each main heading. Bear in mind that the first time you do this, what you write need only be tentative. That doesn't matter: even if it's tentative it will enable you to visualize the essay as a whole early in your writing, and this will help you to judge what to include and what to leave out. Everyone starts with a rough plan and then refines it, so expect your plan to go through several versions.

1. Introduction

A good Introduction will probably have five elements. If each requires no more than a single sentence, you should be able to get them into a single paragraph. The five elements are:

- Context/background. You may feel it's appropriate to begin with a sentence that 'sets the scene', showing you're aware of a current debate or issues, or gives the background to the problem that you're going to address. If you're absolutely certain it would be relevant and appropriate, you could begin with a quotation, but you must be absolutely sure that it is relevant and appropriate. If in doubt, leave it out.

- Interpretation of the topic. Refer back to Chapters 11 and 12 for help with clarifying the topic and avoiding traps. You need to say what you under-stand by any terms that aren't self-explanatory, and to draw attention to anything that a question or statement takes for granted (e.g. implicit assertions and assumptions) and any ambiguities (where the words could have more than one meaning) that need to be resolved in order for you to proceed. Don't stint on words for this. (You can always edit down later if need be.) With a complex topic, you might need an entire paragraph to deal with interpretation alone.

- Methodology. It's a good idea to include just a very brief mention of the methodology you'll be applying or the perspective from which you are approaching the topic. (You'll be giving it a fuller treatment in the methodology section.) A sentence beginning: 'In this essay I shall . . .' (or 'This essay will . . .' if your teachers don't like essays written in the first person) will usually be sufficient. If you're putting forward a proposition, state it here, and outline how you're going to substantiate it.

■ Materials. Include just a very brief mention of the materials you're using, e.g. case studies of X and Y, or key texts (author and title). Again, a single sentence will usually suffice. If you need to say more you can put it in the Materials Used section of the essay.

■ Contents of the essay. Conclude your Introduction with an outline of what's to come in the following sections of the essay: 'In this essay I shall . . .'. And if your teachers like you to say at the outset what your conclusion will be, a sentence beginning 'It will be concluded/shown/argued that . . .' should satisfy them.

As you see, creating an outline of your Introduction is fairly straightforward but it does require you to put in a certain amount of thinking. While you are creating it, you will perhaps want to refer to the texts that you're using – a reminder that reading and writing are not self-contained, mutually exclusive activities: they overlap and intermingle. When you've finished, you'll see how your thinking pays off: you now have a 'launching pad' for your essay. A good launching pad gets your writing off to a good start, especially as it will enable you to see exactly where you're heading.

2. Methodology

A good Methodology section tells the reader, in as few words as possible, *how* you are going to tackle the topic. Your methodology will probably fall into one of the following categories:

■ Using analytical tools. These tools include the definitions, concepts, hypotheses, theories and/or models that you're using; any assumptions that you're making; and the perspective from which you are approaching your subject. Your perspective provides you with 'spectacles' through which you view the subject: certain features will register with you and you'll regard them as significant, while others won't register and so you will in effect treat them as insignificant. Making a note of the analytical tools you're using should pose no difficulty, unless you yourself aren't clear what your way of working is. You *will* have a way of working – unless you're being completely unsystematic – but you haven't made it explicit even to yourself. So try to distance yourself from what you're doing – to 'stand outside' the perspective that you're adopting – to make your methodology explicit.

■ Data gathering and processing. Under this heading come whatever techniques of measurement and quantitative and/or qualitative analysis you are using.

■ Testing against evidence. This involves asking questions such as 'Is this assertion corroborated by the facts?', 'Does my proposition hold for all cases?', 'Is X's hypothesis consistent with the findings of Y's research?', 'Does this model fit the evidence?' and 'Have predictions based on this theory been fulfilled by actual events?'

■ Logical testing. This involves questioning the logic of the statement that you are dealing with and scrutinizing the literature for internal inconsistencies, omissions, defective logic, or bias. If you're testing a proposition of your own, you do the same. You might want to check whether the conclusions that someone has drawn from their study do actually follow from the data that they obtained rather than from assumptions they made at the outset.

■ Comparing and contrasting. Be sure to state clearly the criteria that you are using for this exercise.

■ Synthesizing. You might be aiming to put together your own findings with other findings and facts, opinions and hypotheses from a variety of sources, and thereby synthesize an argument of your own. Say so.

■ Evaluating. Say what value judgments (and whose) you are going to base your evaluation on.

3. Materials Used

Start by making only a brief note of the materials that you'll be using. If you'll be referring to your materials at greater length in the next section of your essay, you needn't go into detail. Here are some categories that you could use:

■ Material that takes the form of original texts that you're using, whether creative, such as works of fiction or academic theorizing, or derivative, such as academic commentary. Say which texts you are using.

■ Empirical evidence. Say what data sources, 'facts', records, observations you are using, and comment on whether they are 'raw' or filtered through the perceptions and judgments of the people providing them. By way of a check, ask yourself, 'What can I be sure that I actually *know* about this topic?'

■ Case studies and other research reports, including inferences drawn by their authors. In addition to citing these, and providing whatever extracts are appropriate, say why you have chosen these particular case studies.

■ Reference materials: relevant knowledge and theory. This will include materials of the kind that can be found in textbooks and reference books (e.g. statutes and law reports in the case of law topics).

■ Other literature. Mention other relevant writings that you have read. If you are compiling a literature review, you may want to include short extracts. (Don't copy out long passages: doing so will not gain you any marks.) Give the gist of what the literature is contributing to your work – concepts to apply, hypotheses to test, questions to answer, disagreements to explore, etc. – but save discussion of it for your Discussion section.

4. Analysis

This is where you show your reasoning, your 'working': you're now applying your methodology to your materials. If this is something your teachers are keen on, it will be worth going into some detail here. So include:

■ Any findings that you can take directly from your material. (To take a simple example, if you have data on road traffic flowing past a certain point for every hour of the day you will probably find that there is an hour of maximum traffic flow and an hour of minimum flow.)

■ Your reasoning. If you have difficulty pinpointing this, as may happen if you are considering, discussing or exploring, write down as much of your analysis as you can, just as it comes into your mind. For a start, simply say what you 'make' of your materials: what you learn from inspecting them, what lessons you think you can draw. Then look at what you have written and highlight words that denote or imply cause and effect: for example, 'cause', 'effect', 'affect', 'makes', 'therefore', 'because', 'consequently', 'so', 'means'. Now go back to each of the sentences that contain those high-lighted words, and spell out the reasoning that you have employed. This will probably take the form of a series of steps. Look at each step closely and aim to satisfy yourself that each one, and the series of steps in total, is rational and logical.

■ Your results: what you get from carrying out your analysis. These will include the results of any calculations, computations and comparisons that you have carried out, the results of any logical testing and testing against evidence that you have done, and the outcomes of any synthesis and evaluation that you have performed.

5. Discussion

If your results fall into a number of parts, or 'strands', your Discussion will usually draw them together and consider them in their entirety. It could cover:

■ The validity of your results. What confidence do you have in them? Are they universally valid? How far can one safely generalize from them? Are there certain problems that you faced in applying your methodology that are worth mentioning? (Your teacher might be particularly interested in what you have to say about this.)

■ The implications of your results. These might include (a) their immediate significance (what can be learned from them); (b) their wider significance, e.g. for future developments in the field; for research; and for the policies and practices of government bodies, non-governmental organizations, and businesses; (c) judgments that you have reached, e.g. as to how society as a whole or different groups of people are being or will be affected, and whether the impact on these groups will be good or bad; (d) any recommendations that you are making, e.g. what steps – if any – should be taken by government or other bodies.

■ Comments on and critiques of theories, propositions, etc. that you encountered in the literature.

■ If you have been asked to discuss a statement, you will need to set out the conditions under which it holds ('is true'), or the qualifications or limitations that you feel must be attached to it ('it depends').

In creating your Discussion you should always bear in mind that you are writing for another human being, the person who will read your essay. So try to put yourself in that person's shoes. An essay intended for your teacher might be written with a view to satisfying certain marking criteria, but if you were aiming to write a piece worthy of being submitted to an academic journal, you'd ask yourself what would hold a professional reader's attention, and the requirements would not be the same. If you've been asked to imagine that you're a consultant writing a report for the chief executive of a large company or public body, you would not be exploring interesting side issues and your Conclusions (see below) would probably take the form of bullet-pointed recommendations.

6. Conclusions

There are some basic rules for writing Conclusions to an essay:

- They should be clear and pithy. It's possible that the marker will turn to them immediately after reading the Introduction, so they should not be untidy and weak or give the impression that you lost interest when writing or that you finished the essay in a great rush.

- They should incorporate the briefest possible summary of your Discussion. Include the salient points only. You won't earn any marks for repeating what you've already written in your Discussion.

- Never, ever introduce new material in your Conclusions. If it's worth including, it should appear in your Materials Used section and feature in your Discussion.

- Do revisit your starting point. Your Conclusions and Introduction must match up. So if your topic took the form of a direct question, which you will have detailed in your Introduction, in your Conclusions you should summarize in one or two sentences your answer to it. If you were given a statement or proposition to discuss, set out in your Conclusions the view you have formed on it. And if the reader will expect recommendations, don't forget to include these.

A final thought. As ever, please regard the above as suggestions to help you create an essay plan, not as the definitive last word on how to do it. Treat them as a stimulus, not as a straightjacket. There *are* different ways of doing it: see pages 118–9 for an example.

19

Titles, abstracts, executive summaries and appendices

Titles, abstracts, executive summaries and appendices are ancillary 'extras' to essays. You may be required to submit an abstract or executive summary with your essay, while an appendix is something that you may find it convenient to employ.

Titles

If you have been given a topic for your essay, that topic will serve as its title. You mess with it at your peril, because you run the risk of distorting the topic and ending up writing an essay that misses its point or some of its aspects.

If you have to compose your own title, try to come up with one that is succinct but at the same time informative. If you have been given a subject to write about, your title could be that subject. For example, if you have been told to write about one of Charlotte Brontë's novels, your subject could simply be 'Jane Eyre'. More informatively, it could be something like 'Charlotte Brontë's treatment of friendship in *Jane Eyre*' or '*Jane Eyre*: a comparative analysis of male–female relationships'. Note how the use of the colon allows you to include both context and methodology in your title: this device is much used by academic writers, and you should feel free to use it yourself.

Abstracts

An abstract of an essay or paper is a synopsis – a brief summary – of what it contains. It comes in front of the essay, so it's the first thing the reader will see. The purpose of an abstract is to enable the reader to get an idea of what is in the essay without actually going to the trouble of reading it. (Your department may require you to submit an abstract so that the essay may be passed to the most appropriate person for marking.) You'll almost certainly be given a word limit, typically in the range 150–300 words.

You will find it easiest to compose your abstract when you have completed the essay, although if at any time you find you're getting bogged down in the writing process it may be helpful to have a shot at writing an abstract as a way of getting your mind into 'overview mode' and visualizing the essay as a whole.

If you have written an Introduction and Conclusion on the lines suggested in Chapter 18, you can probably put together a good enough abstract by taking from them most – if not all – of what you need: a sentence each on context/background, methodology and materials from your Introduction, and one or two sentences from your Conclusions. To make a better job of it, ask yourself what would appeal to the person who's going to read it. If that person is someone who doesn't know the field well, you may want to say more about the background or context. If it's someone who is particularly interested in methodology, or in the materials you've used, say a little more about those aspects. Above all, highlight in your abstract anything that you feel is special, that shows originality, insight, lateral thinking or breadth of knowledge. Think of your abstract as an advertisement for your essay: you want to show off its best points!

In some circumstances you may have to submit an abstract before you have written the essay. If the essay is to be an extended piece of work, you may be required to do so in order that a suitable person can be allocated as your supervisor. If you hope to be invited to present your work in person at a conference or colloquium, the organizers will want to see your abstract before deciding whether to invite you or not. Follow the same recipe as you would if the essay already existed: background/context, methodology, materials, conclusion. And think carefully about what would appeal to the organizers and fit into the programme they envisage.

Executive summaries

You may be asked to produce an executive summary if you have written a report on a project of some kind, especially if you've written it from the point of view of a consultant writing for a client. Like an abstract, the executive summary comes at the front of the report. Its purpose is to enable the reader to see at a glance what the main points of the report are. It usually takes the form not of a dense paragraph, like an abstract, but of a list of bullet points. Readability is crucial. Your executive summary should be all on one page, in a reasonably large font (not less than 12 pt). It could look like this:

■ Background to the problem

■ How you studied the problem: techniques used, data collected, etc.

- Analysis: causes of the problem, what the data show

- Alternative solutions (shortlist)

- Criteria for choosing between alternative solutions

- Pros and cons of each alternative solution

- Recommended solution.

A good executive summary thus enables the reader not only to see your main points at a glance: he or she can follow your reasoning step by logical step, and challenge it at any point. Note how this list adapts the essay structure offered in Chapter 18. It takes only the background from the Introduction; the Methodology and Materials Used sections are combined; the Discussion section is broken down into three constituent parts; and the recommended solution only is taken from the Conclusions.

As you can see, the essence of an executive summary is that it is *practical*. Bear in mind that you may be writing for someone to whom the word 'academic' is a pejorative term, a synonym for impractical, 'airy-fairy' and irrelevant. Adapt your mindset accordingly!

Appendices

Appendices are not often advocated for student essays, but they can come in very handy. For example, you may have a quantity of data that you feel it is essential to present but to do so would result in your essay having a large, indigestible chunk at its very centre. Rather than omit these data you can put them in an appendix. Then they won't interrupt the flow of the essay but are available for the reader to consult if he or she wishes to – if only to be sure that you didn't invent them!

An appendix can also come in handy when you are pursuing a side issue. For example, you may have encountered certain problems with your methodology and feel that they deserve to be discussed, but to do so would constitute a distraction from the line of reasoning that you're pursuing. Get around this problem by putting that discussion in an appendix.

20

How to use quotations

Quotations from primary sources

When you want to quote from something you've found in a piece of original writing (i.e. it's not a quotation that the writer has got from someone else), please think about what you want to use the quotation *for*. Ask what it will contribute to your essay. Many student essays simply prefix a quotation with the words 'According to X, . . .' or 'X states . . .' and fail to make clear the *significance* of the quotation, leaving the reader wondering 'So what?' (And as we saw in Chapter 10, it's possible to do this in such a way as to positively mislead the reader.) A good essay *does* make the significance of a quotation clear, and this has a three-fold payoff: in thinking about significance you develop your skill in reasoning and critical thinking; you demonstrate to the reader that you have put thought into the essay; and you are helping to insure yourself against the danger of plagiarism because the thoughts are your own.

The contribution made by a quotation may take one of a variety of types: facts, perceptions, figures of speech, definitions, assumptions, propositions, opinions, value judgments, claims, questions and reasoning. As shown in Table 11, each type of contribution (a) needs to be referred to in a particular way; and (b) invites you to ask certain questions about it.

Table 11 Using quotations

Type of contribution	How to refer to it	Questions to ask about it
Fact	X found, discovered, revealed, ascertained, notes, points out that	Is this fact universally accepted, accurate (so far as you can tell)? Have other significant facts been ignored? How am I using this fact?
Perception	X describes, identifies, distinguishes, categorizes; as X sees it, . . .	Does X have a particular standpoint which causes him/her to perceive things in this particular way? Are there alternative standpoints?
Figure of speech	X regards . . . as; compares . . . to; suggests that . . . is like	Is this an appropriate metaphor or simile? How does it assist my understanding? Do I want to adopt it?[1]
Definition	X defines . . . to mean	Do other writers have different definitions, i.e. attribute different meanings to the same term?
Assumption	X assumes, postulates, hypothesizes, conjectures, takes it for granted that	Do other writers make this assumption? Is it valid, justified? Do I wish to share it? If I make different assumptions, would I come to different conclusions?
Proposition	X proposes, argues, asserts, contends, suggests, hypothesizes . . . that if A, then B; X supports, is critical of, criticizes	How can I test the validity of this proposition, whether it 'fits the facts'?
Opinion	According to X; X tells us, says, thinks, suggests, considers, comments, agrees that; X disagrees with; in X's opinion; it seems to X that	On what grounds (evidence) does X base his opinions? Do other people hold them? If not, why not? Do I agree with X?

Value judgment	To X, it should, ought; to X it is good, bad, beneficial, harmful	Do other people share X's value judgments? Why should I pay attention to them?
Claim	X claims that; in X's professional judgment; to X, it surely, must be, is obvious that; it cannot be; common sense dictates	What is the authority on which X bases his/her claim? Why shouldn't I challenge that claim and authority?
Question	X asks/questions whether	Are these questions relevant? Are there other questions that I ought to be asking?
Reasoning	X infers from this evidence that; shows from his/her analysis that; X demonstrates how; concludes	Is this reasoning sound? Could other conclusions be drawn from the same evidence?

Quotations from secondary sources

You'll often come across a text in which author X gives a quotation from a text by another author, Y, and you feel it's such an appropriate quotation that you want to use it yourself. How should you do this? In an ideal world, you would look up Y's original text so you actually have the primary source to go on. (You will sometimes find that author X has actually misquoted or misunderstood what author Y wrote, or that the quotation carries with it some qualification that X has overlooked, so it really is always worth checking if you can.) But your world may not be ideal: you may not have access to Y's original text, or you may have run out of time.

In that case, first of all check that author X has properly referenced the quotation and has paid proper attention to its significance: for example, has not referred to Y as stating a fact when Y was clearly expressing an opinion. If all is in order, you can write 'X cites Y's finding that . . .' or 'Y's description of . . .' or 'Y's opinion that . . .' and so on. If, on the other hand, X has misrepresented Y, you could point this out (you should get credit for doing so) and then treat the quotation from X in accordance with the formulae offered in Table 11.

Whatever you do, *never* pretend that you have read the original, primary text if you actually haven't. Not only is it poor academic practice, but your teacher may well be familiar with it and there is a good chance that you will be found out.

21

The drawbacks of model essays

Students often ask to see model essays, a very understandable reaction to a situation in which you are required to do something – write an essay – that you haven't actually been taught to do. If you have access to model essays – which, if provided by your teacher or department, will usually be essays that students before you have written – you should be aware of the following drawbacks associated with using them:

■ No model essay is perfect. But you probably won't be able to see the comments that the marker has made on the model, so you run the risk of repeating the original author's faults.

■ You may not be aware of the topic set for the essay or – if you are aware of it – the topic you're working on may be different. Following the model may lead you astray.

■ A submitted essay is a finished piece of work. You won't be aware of the process that produced it. Unless there is a detailed Methodology section, you won't learn about the way the author worked.

■ Your thinking gets 'blinkered'. The more closely you study the model essay, the more difficult you will find it to think differently and produce something different. That way you risk being seduced into plagiarizing the model essay.

What, then, can you usefully do with a model essay? Here are a couple of suggestions:

■ Get hold of more than one model essay. (Check that they are on precisely the same topic as the one you are tackling.) You run less risk of your thinking becoming blinkered if you can see that there are different ways of approaching the topic.

■ Learn as much as you can about the original authors' methodology. Notice the structure of each essay. If the model essays are organized in sections, with headings (and even sub-headings), pay close attention to these. There is no prohibition against copying someone else's structure: just make sure your headings are appropriate to *your* essay rather than to a different one.

22

The process of writing

Writing-as-thinking

There is more than one kind of writing. There is an important distinction to be made between 'writing-as-thinking' and 'writing-as-presenting'. You're doing the former when you're making rough notes, getting down your ideas and sorting them out; and you're doing the latter when you are assembling and finalizing your essay with a reader in mind.

There's another important point to make now. *Writing-as-thinking is for your eyes only.* When you're doing it, do not give a moment's thought to what someone else might think of what you are writing. Correcting and editing and polishing your prose will come later, when you move into writing-as-presenting mode.

Putting your first draft together

Let's say you've already done some targeted reading, highlighted and perhaps made notes on passages that seemed significant, jotted down various thoughts and ideas that have occurred to you, and produced a rough plan for your essay. Now you can begin fitting it all together. Collect your reading matter for the essay and spread it around you. Locate any notes that you've made, your annotated photocopies, and your books and articles bristling with Post-its. Spread them around you too. If you have some flipchart paper handy, stick your plan in the middle of a sheet and your Post-its and notes around it.

You are now ready to start fitting your notes into your essay plan. See which of them obviously belong under particular headings or sub-headings. If any of them don't, this might mean either that they don't belong anywhere in this essay, and so should be discarded, or that you need to invent a new heading or sub-heading to go in your plan. Feel free to revise your plan as and when necessary: remember that your plan is an aid to thinking, not a straightjacket which your thoughts have to be forced into.

When you have a rough idea where everything goes, you can start writing –

working up your notes into a rough first draft. You don't need to do this in any particular order: you might like to tackle the trickiest section first. Think of the various sections of your essay as 'growing up' together. Do avoid spending a lot of time on your Introduction: you will certainly want to amend it when you have finalized your Conclusions, because Introduction and Conclusions must 'match up'. And again, bear in mind that your first draft is for your eyes only: it'll be rough, and that's fine!

Monitoring your progress

Every decent essay goes through a succession of drafts before it is finally submitted. This is perfectly normal, and it's a process with which academics are very familiar. Computers with word-processing software make it very easy to save a draft and proceed to develop the next version (see below).

Do monitor your progress. By this I mean:

■ Keep an eye on your word count.

Students have been known to find themselves already over their word limit with half the essay still to write, and the deadline approaching. Don't let this happen to you.

■ Check regularly that you're 'on track'.

If you ever get the feeling that the essay is 'diverging' – broadening out – rather than 'converging', coming together as you get closer to your Conclusions, see if there is any point that is reasonably self-contained and that you could accordingly leave out without weakening the essay. (Yes, it can be very painful to discard material that you have worked hard on. Could you attach it to your essay as an appendix? Or might it come in handy when you're revising for exams?)

■ Monitor the 'shape' of your essay.

Every essay has a 'shape', which can be described in terms of the proportion of the total number of words taken up by each section. Thus, most 2,000-word essays would probably be made up of sections like this:

○ Introduction: 150–200 words (7½–10 per cent)

○ Methodology: 200–300 words (10–15 per cent)

○ Materials Used: 100–200 words (5-10 per cent)

○ Analysis: 400–600 words (20–30 per cent)

○ Discussion: 250–750 words (12½–37½ per cent)

○ Conclusions: 150–200 words (7½–10 per cent).

Most academics will be accustomed to shapes like these, so it would be sensible for your essay to conform to this convention. If it looks as though it won't conform, check whether you seem to be writing too little or too much in any of the six sections.

Of course, it could be that you are adopting a well-known methodology about which there is very little to say, or that you are giving a detailed description of the materials you've used in your Analysis section and so need say little about them in your Materials Used section, so these sections will justifiably be 'undersized'. Or it could be that one of your sections is very big, in which case you can divide it into two parts. Otherwise, see whether you need to strengthen the undersized sections and cut down the oversized ones. Make such changes sooner rather than later.

■ Monitor your structure regularly.

Because you have been thinking while you have been writing, it would not be surprising to find that you have introduced new questions halfway through the essay, thereby destroying your structure. Promote these questions to your Introduction and redo your structure. Or you might have altered your methodology, in which case you should review it and make consequential amendments elsewhere. Or perhaps your Conclusions, if you have started drafting them, don't actually answer the topic set: either review them immediately to bring them into line, or go back to your Introduction and reinterpret the topic.

■ Monitor your alertness and allow yourself time.

Essay writing demands concentration on your part. It's certainly hard work. Once you get into the swing of it you'll probably be surprised by the length of time you can keep going. Nevertheless, there will be times when your head swims and you feel it's all becoming a terrible burden. When this happens, take a break! Go for a walk, do some housework, get yourself some refreshment, play some music.

When we are thinking hard, the process may seem to be very much a conscious and rational one, like carrying out calculations. But bear in mind that there's a subconscious process going on as well. Ideas will 'pop into your head' and 'dawn on you': your mind has a mind of its own, so to speak! This process can't be hurried (although brainstorming can help – see the next chapter) so you need to allow time for it. That's a good reason for starting work on your essay in good time.

Writing-as-presenting

Now it's time to get down to some serious writing: assembling and editing for presentation. You have the job of turning your notes into sentences and paragraphs with proper English grammar and correct spelling. You can work on sections in any order. You may want to get some or all sections written up in rough form, and then polish them all at one go later. It's up to you: there is no one right way of doing it.

You may be told that a well-written essay has a smooth 'flow': each paragraph or each section leads on logically to the next. I would endorse this, but it isn't always easy to achieve. An essay has to be linear in form – each paragraph has only one before it and only one following it – whereas the thinking that you want to present may be in your head as a cloud or network of interconnected points.

Problems arise when you've spent a paragraph going into detail: in effect, you've gone down a branch line, and now have to decide how you are going to take your reader back on to the main track. And when you've had to write something about each of several points or case studies 'in parallel', as it were, you need to find a way of taking your reader smoothly forward after dealing with the last one.

The solution to these problems lies in making it crystal clear to the reader what you are doing. Provide a contents list for your essay, with sub-headings and lists. Material under a sub-heading doesn't have to lead on to material under the next main heading: the reader won't expect it to, and won't be 'thrown' when it doesn't. And to get back on track after you've worked your way through several parallel points or case studies, it's a good idea to have a sentence or two drawing the separate strands together: by giving a summary or overview, for example. Such 'signposts' and 'navigational sentences' are particularly desirable if your teachers don't like to see headings and sub-headings in your essays.

Finally, note that when you're assembling and editing your essay with your reader in mind, it is perfectly possible that you may see mistakes and lapses in your reasoning that had escaped you before. This is quite usual, so don't give yourself a hard time if it happens to you. Deal with it by going back to writing-as-thinking mode: make some rough notes, sort out what you really want to say, and then go back to writing for presentation. All academic writing emerges from a cyclical process of this kind.

Writing to a word limit: the breadth-versus-depth dilemma

If you have to write an essay that must not exceed a certain number of words, you may be faced with a dilemma. You don't know whether to deal with the topic broadly and not go into depth, or to deal with it narrowly but in depth: you can't do both. In effect, you have to make a trade-off between breadth and depth.

The problem is that taking the broad approach could lead you to write in generalities and broad generalizations, and lead to your essay being marked down as being too shallow, too superficial. Almost certainly your teacher will be looking for some depth in what you write. This could involve not so much providing detail but showing that you have some insight into the subject (you are aware of its subtleties, such as fine variations, dependence on the particular circumstances of a situation, or possible errors or biases on the part of writers whom you've consulted) and/or showing that you have a grasp of the analytical methods required for an in-depth treatment.

Having said this, there is one sensible precaution to take. You need to show the reader that you are aware of the breadth of the subject and that you have made your selection of areas within the topic consciously – after some thought – rather than written about one or two areas because they're the only ones you know about.

So you might select three writers, or three case studies, because they illustrate two extremes and a mid-point. Having made your selection, be sure to tell your reader early in the essay – e.g. in your Introduction – what you have done, and why.

It probably hasn't escaped you that the breadth-versus-depth dilemma applies on a wider scale to many (if not all) of the courses you are taking, especially if you are faced with monster reading lists. If you have accustomed yourself to combining an 'overview' approach with selective in-depth treatment of topics you will have gone a long way towards mastering the subject – and preparing yourself for exams too. But because teaching in higher education is such a personal matter, it would be prudent to find out whether your teachers disagree with any of this advice, and, if so, on what grounds.

Using a computer

Computers have made essay writing much easier than in the past. You can save your notes in a convenient format, work them up into proper sentences and paragraphs without starting afresh, use software to add footnotes, and experiment with different structures for an essay. When writing an essay, there are three particular rules to follow:

- Save your work frequently. Get into the habit of saving it every time you pause to think: it soon becomes something you do automatically.

- Back up your work whenever you take a break. Save the essay not only in your personal folder but also on a flash drive. Open an account with Google mail so you can email your essay to yourself and find it whenever you want by going to your mail account.

- Incorporate a 'version number' in your essay's file name, e.g. 'Industrialization v05.doc'. Then each time you return to your essay after backing it up, open the document and immediately save it with a new version number (so 'Industrialization v05.doc' becomes 'Industrialization v06.doc'). By doing this you retain all the previous versions and can return to any of them if the need arises.

Writing style and language

Don't write like a textbook! There is one feature of academics' writing and lecturing that you should not try to imitate: the 'authority' with which they sometimes imbue their material. An academic may use authority-implying expressions such as 'We consider . . .', 'In our judgment, . . .', 'As so-and-so rightly says, . . .'. All these expressions carry the implication that he or she is an authority on the subject and not to be challenged. If you, as a student, use them, what you say and write will strike your teachers as pretentious and inappropriate.

Some teachers have very definite views about style, and may mark your work down if they disapprove of yours. So, before submitting an essay to anyone, or making a presentation in their presence, you should feel free to ask them any or all of the following questions:

- Is it acceptable for me to write in the first person, for example 'In this essay I shall show . . .', 'I feel . . .' and 'I conclude . . .'? Or do you prefer impersonal forms, such as 'This essay will show . . .', 'The present writer feels . . .' and 'One would conclude . . .'?

- Do you prefer essays to be written in the passive voice, for example 'A study was made by X' and 'It was felt . . .'? Or may I use the active voice: 'X made a study' and (if the first person usage is permitted) 'I felt . . .'?

- Is it acceptable to use headings and sub-headings in my essays? (Some teachers feel that these interfere with the flow of the prose.)

- Is it acceptable to make use of case studies or other materials that weren't on the reading list but I found for myself?

- Will I be penalized for spelling mistakes in essays or for using the American spellings for words?

- Will I be penalized if I express views that disagree with yours?

I offer you these suggestions as a matter of practical politics, in recognition of the fact that, as a student, you are situated at a low level in a power structure, and that it is a power structure in which language is used to claim and assert authority. Have you encountered that expression beloved of academics 'The evidence suggests . . .'? Evidence on its own suggests nothing whatever, of course. The accurate expression would be 'On the basis of this evidence I think that . . .'. But in the culture of UK higher education, to use such language would amount to an abdication of authority.

In the interests of user-friendliness, I have written this book using the informal, colloquial language of spoken English as much as possible – expressions such as 'bits' and 'a lot', for example. There are two dangers that you may encounter if you do this in academic writing: it may lead you to be imprecise, and it may give the impression that you are sloppy and non-rigorous – even journalistic (a term of abuse in some academic circles) – in the way that you think. I suggest, therefore, that you avoid the following words and expressions (possible alternatives are given in brackets):

'it's' (it is). Avoid *all* such contractions

'bits' (parts)

'things' (units, elements, factors)

'a couple of' (two)

'a lot' or 'a load' (a considerable/significant/sizeable amount, number or quantity)

'like' (similar to, such as, as though)

'get' (obtain, become)

'as well as' (in addition to)

'How come . . .?' (What caused . . .? What brought about . . .?)

'means that' (results in, has the consequence that)

'the reason why X happened' (the cause of X happening. Reasons exist only in people's minds, so don't say things like 'the reason why the car broke down'.)

'you are' (one is). *Never* address an academic reader as 'you'.

The rule is: avoid 'chatty', conversational language!

A whole book could be written about how to write in clear, grammatically correct English for academic readers. Fortunately such a book has already been written: I suggest you get hold of Christine Sinclair's *Grammar: A Friendly Approach* (Open University Press, 2007) if you encounter any criticism of your use of English. It's full of clear advice and very readable.

23

Writer's block and how to overcome it

So-called writer's block is not restricted to students: it's a common affliction among professional writers too. They can't get started on a piece of work, or they sit and stare at the computer screen for hours, or go off and do other things. (Students tend to go off and do more reading.) Being told to stop procrastinating doesn't help in the slightest.

If this applies to you, I wonder what's going on. Perhaps there's something on your mind, a worry of some kind, or a more urgent task that you need to be getting on with. Perhaps a bit of you really does not want to be doing this piece of writing, and you're doing more reading as a 'displacement activity', to put off starting. Or perhaps your subconscious mind is busy sorting out what you've read and processing it, and doesn't want to be interrupted. If your block is making you anxious, your anxiety may be getting in the way of resuming your normal writing activity.

There could be other factors at work, however. Perhaps you simply do not know any techniques for getting started: maybe no one has taken the trouble to teach them to you. Perhaps you're trying to put perfectly formed sentences on to the page from the very start. This course of action is bound to lead to frustration, because you are trying to do two incompatible things simultaneously: you're trying to brainstorm and to edit at the same time. Or perhaps your thinking is in a rut: you've met an obstacle and are repeatedly trying to bash your way through it rather than thinking of ways round it, so it feels as if you're banging your head on a brick wall!

So what you should do? Here are some ideas. All you need to try them out is a quiet place in which to work, a supply of clean A4 paper and preferably some pens with inks in a variety of colours. (Alternatively you could use a pad of flipchart paper and a stack of Post-it notes.) There are four different techniques that you can adopt: all of them involve a form of brainstorming. You can:

■ Begin at the beginning

■ Work backwards from the end

■ Create a 'question string'

■ Turn work into play.

Begin at the beginning

The beginning is your topic. Copy it out in the middle of a sheet of paper and put it on your desk or table in front of you so you can see it easily. Now take five sheets of paper and at the top of each one write down one of the five elements of an Introduction (see pages 90–91): (1) Context/background, (2) Interpretation, (3) Methodology, (4) Materials, (5) Outline of the essay (Contents).

On sheet 1 write down three or four interesting things about the background to the topic, or the context in which it belongs. Do this quickly. What you write should be descriptive and factual, so shouldn't require much thought. Use different coloured pens for each item. On sheet 2 make a list of the significant words and phrases in the topic, then by each one write the meaning (or meanings if there's more than one) that you think each has. If the topic is in the form of a statement which you have to discuss, see if you can express it in the form of a question. Again, use a range of colours and try to do this quickly: you can always come back to it and improve it later. Now turn to sheet 3 and quickly jot down the steps you need to take to reach a conclusion. If your topic is a question (or you've turned it into one), jot down the steps you think you probably ought to take to arrive at the answer to it. If your topic is (or started out as) a statement, jot down the steps you think you probably ought to take in order to discover whether the statement is accurate, valid or 'true'. On sheet 4 make a multi-coloured list of the information that you have about the topic. Don't write anything out in full: very brief notes will do. Leave sheet 5 blank for the moment.

While you're working, do not – repeat NOT – attempt to edit or censor yourself. Don't spend a single moment wondering what other people would make of your efforts. This exercise is all about using writing to aid your thinking process. What you write down is for your eyes only. It's nothing to do with presentation.

You should now have a sizeable – and interesting, and satisfying – collection of jottings. Why not take a break now (overnight is fine)? When you return to your task, review your collection. Discard notes and listed items that you can't see yourself using. Now remind yourself about the archetypal essay structure – Introduction/Methodology/Materials Used/Analysis/Discussion/Conclusions –

and try to fit your remaining notes and items into it. Remember not to treat that structure as a straightjacket: modify the structure to fit your notes, etc., not the other way round. In essence you're looking for a logical sequence. When you've done this, you should have a first draft of the outline of your essay, and you can put this on sheet 5.

Now take or make a sentence from each of your sheets 1–5. Put them together on another sheet in a single paragraph, and hey presto!, you now have an Introduction. It may be rough and ready, and you'll almost certainly want to improve it later on, but you've made a start: you now have a 'launching pad' for your essay.

Work backwards from the end

It's an experience common to most writers that at some point they get bogged down – writing becomes slow and a chore – or feel they've gone off track. If you get to this point, stop what you're doing. Turn to a clean page – paper or screen – and start jotting down rough notes on your *conclusions*. Again you're brainstorming, so just write down whatever comes into your head. You don't need to justify what you write: just get it down! The point here is that almost certainly you have ideas floating around in your subconscious mind about what your conclusions will be – your answer to a direct question, your views on a statement, for example – and this is a way of fetching them into the daylight. Do this quickly, then take a break, and then go back to them. See if they form obvious groups or clusters, or if you can assemble them into a logical list. You may want to improve some of them at this stage, but don't try to edit or polish them.

What this exercise does is help you to focus on the end point of your writing process. You're still writing-as-thinking, but whereas before you were heading out into the desert without a map, so to speak, now you have some idea of your destination. You might want to modify that destination later, but even so you now have at least a sense of direction.

Once you've done this, go back to the beginning of your essay and review the notes you've already written. Keep the ones that are pointing in the direction of your destination, and jettison any that are pointing down a side road. You should now find it easier to progress in the direction you want to go in.

Create a 'question string'

There's another approach which can be applied both to statements that you are required to discuss and to direct questions (the ones with a question mark at the end). The approach amounts to 'exploding' the statement or question into a number of questions.[1] Here is an example which starts with a statement:

'Anti-poverty policies can never succeed.' Discuss.

Your 'question string' might look like this:

- What is meant by 'poverty'?

- What is meant by an 'anti-poverty policy'?

- What criteria of success can I use? (For example, whether outcomes match intentions)

- Do I want to restrict my answer geographically (to a locality, region, country or continent)?

- What case studies can I use?

- What information do I have about the form that anti-poverty policies take or have taken? (Statements of intention/legislation/allocation of resources, etc.)

- What were the actual intentions of the 'policy makers'?

- How were the policies implemented?

- What were the outcomes?

- Did the outcomes match the intentions?

- Has there been more success in some cases than others?

- How can variations be explained? (Lack of resources/lack of political will/ local factors affecting implementation, etc.)

- Which of these can be characterized as 'impediments to success'?

- Under what circumstances/conditions are these impediments less likely to occur/more likely to be easily overcome?

- What are the policy implications of my findings?

As you can see, the topic has been 'translated' into fifteen succinct and straightforward 'sub-questions'. Once you have identified these sub-questions, you have a structure for your essay. Answer them in turn and there's your essay!

You can also use your list of questions to put together a neat little introduction, perhaps on the following lines:

> A number of Western governments have adopted domestic anti-poverty policies, and – in conjunction with certain international bodies – policies aimed at relieving poverty in so-called Third World countries. [*Background/context*] In this essay I shall first consider the problematic terms in the proposition that 'Anti-poverty policies can never succeed'. [*Interpretation*] I shall then examine some examples of anti-poverty policies drawn from different parts of the world [*Materials*], paying attention to the intentions behind them, the measures employed, and the outcomes achieved. [*Methodology*] I shall show that in some/many/ most cases, outcomes fell short of publicized intentions. I shall then identify and discuss the factors that contributed to these shortfalls, and set out the implications of my findings for future anti-poverty policies. [*Outline*, which in this case actually starts from 'In this essay . . .']

If, after drawing up your list of sub-questions, you realize there are some that you can't answer, be aware that you have done something extremely useful: you have identified a gap in your knowledge. It's your cue to do a bit more targeted reading, and to look through your books, photocopies, lecture notes, etc. for the specific material you need.

Turn work into play

By and large, academic work is a serious business. The problem this creates is that you can easily get caught up in the seriousness of it, and this can repress your subconscious mind and stop ideas bubbling up. So take time out to play with your topic. Turn statements into direct questions, and direct questions into statements. Play with the words: change them and move them around. Turn statements or questions into jokes: it will do wonders for you in terms of relaxing your mind and giving rein to your imagination and creativity if you can turn a topic into a joke that makes you laugh.

I used this method myself on occasion when writing this book. (You may be able to guess where.) Anyone can do it. Including you!

Part 4
Referencing styles

24

How to use and cite sources

Using other people's writings as sources and acknowledging their contribution by 'citing' the source – i.e. supplying a reference to it – is central to academic writing. Citing your sources is not only a way of providing you with an important protection against being accused of plagiarism, it is also good academic practice. It shows a proper concern on your part with the quality of the evidence you have used and with substantiating your conclusion. In any worthwhile essay that you write, your reasoning will involve making use of what others before you have written. Citing your sources will enable the reader to check that you have used those sources appropriately and that your reasoning is sound. This is the intellectual – as opposed to the self-protective – justification for citing your sources.

Using and citing sources requires you to provide three things:

■ Within your essay, an extract from the source (a word-for-word quotation or your own paraphrase of a quotation) or a statement of your own to which the source is relevant

■ Within your essay, an insert of some kind in the text: a cue or 'signpost' that directs the reader to a place where details of the source can be found

■ A list of the details of all of your sources (see Chapter 26).

Incorporating extracts into your text

Short extracts

If you are quoting directly (rather than paraphrasing), and the extract is not more than a certain length – this could be two lines, three lines, 30 words or 40 words: check with whatever referencing style guide you're using (see below) – enclose it in quotation marks. Check with your style guide too to see whether these should be single or double quotation marks. If the extract already includes a word, phrase or sentence in quotation marks, the guide may tell you that these should be double if the 'outside' ones are single, and vice versa.

Longer extracts

If your extract is longer than two or three lines, indent it. Your style guide may tell you whether it should be indented from both margins or only the left-hand margin. An indented extract should not be enclosed in quotation marks.

Shortened extracts

It is permissible to shorten an extract by taking out words, as long as you do not change the author's meaning. (Never remove the word 'not', for example!) The fact that words have been taken out is shown by the insertion of (usually) three dots (i.e. full stops, or periods). Your own words can be inserted in place of the author's: this is usually done so that the extract still reads grammatically. Your own words should be enclosed in square brackets and again you must not change the author's meaning. If, as a result of your shortening, a word that was formerly inside a sentence now begins one, the first letter of that word may be enclosed in square brackets. (Again, consult your style guide: it may or may not require this.)

Paraphrasing

If you are paraphrasing someone else's work, it is important to make it clear that you are doing so: use some formula such as 'To paraphrase X, . . .', 'X appears to be assuming/arguing/suggesting . . .', 'in other words . . .' (after an actual quotation).

The bewildering variety of referencing styles

Please note that there is no single right way of referencing. Ask your teachers if they have preferences as to which referencing style you should use, *and* either to supply you with a style guide or refer you to one. In some fields (e.g. law, medicine) there are standard styles in the UK and USA and other English-speaking countries, but in others there are not. Some publishers and journals have their own distinctive house style, too. As a second best, ask your teachers to suggest a book or a journal whose style you can follow.

There are, as far as I can see, four kinds of referencing style in general use. You can easily tell which is being used in a book or article that you're reading because they have different kinds of insert in the text. Look out for the following:

- Author and date, e.g. Smith (1980) or (Smith, 1980). Full details of Smith's 1980 publication are contained in a list at the end of the book, the chapter or the article. I refer to this as the **author/date** style.

- Author and page number, e.g. Jones (117) or (Jones 117). I refer to this as the **author/page** style.

- Superscript, e.g. [12]. The superscript, or raised number, directs you to a footnote (at the foot of the page) or endnote (at the end of the book, chapter or article) with the same number. Full details of the publication are contained in the footnote or endnote. I refer to this as the **numbered-note** style. (The British Standards Institution publication BS 5605:1990 *Recommendations for Citing and Referencing Published Material* (BSI, 1990) describes it as the 'running notes' method.) It is the style used in this book.

- Bracketed numbers, e.g. (12). Like the numbered-note style, the bracketed number directs you to a footnote (at the foot of the page) or endnote (at the end of the book, chapter or article) with the same number. The best-known version of this is the Vancouver style, but you'll also find it referred to as the 'numeric' style, so I refer to it as the **Vancouver-numeric** style. Unlike the numbered-note style, the same number – bracketed – may appear in more than one place in the text.

25

Which style to choose?

If you have an essay to write, and you have some choice when it comes to selecting a referencing style, which one should you choose? Here are some things you should know about the four main kinds:

The author/date style

Varieties

In the UK and Australia the most common version of the author/date style is that known as the Harvard style. In the USA the well-known APA, ASA/ASR and CBE and AIP styles are versions of the author/date style.[1] It is commonly used in the physical and life sciences and the social sciences.

Inserts in the text

In the text you place an insert giving the author(s) and date of publication. For example: 'Smith (1980) describes X as . . .' or 'X has been described (Smith, 1980) as . . .'. If Smith had two publications in 1980, they are differentiated by putting letters (a, b) after the year. So if you are referring to both at different places, your text with inserts would look something like: 'Smith (1980a) describes . . .' and 'Smith (1980b) concludes . . .'. You might also want or be required to include page numbers, so that the reader does not have to wade through Smith's book in its entirety to find your source. Then your text with inserts would look something like: 'Smith (1980a, p. 13) describes . . .' or 'Some writers have concluded (e.g. Smith, 1980b: 17–18) . . .'. Your style guide should tell you whether you are required to prefix page numbers by p. (for a single page) or pp. (for more than one page), and whether it should be '(Smith, 1980)' or '(Smith 1980)'.

Listing

For every different insert, you write a reference saying where the source can be found. At the end of your essay you attach a list of all the references, in alphabetical order of authors' surnames. This list might be headed 'Bibliography', 'List of references' or 'Works cited'. There are a number of ways in which entries in the list could be set out – different style manuals prescribe different ones – but they all have in common that they begin something like: 'Smith, T. (1980) . . .'.

Usefulness

The author/date style is most useful where all your sources are books or journal articles with one or more designated authors. The insertion of dates in the text may be helpful, as Ritter points out, for following the progress of a debate.[2] This style also allows you to add or subtract references easily if you need to amend your essay just before handing it in. It is less useful if you have to deal with 'messy' sources like newspaper articles and editorials, the publications of government bodies or other organizations where no author is credited, broadcasts on TV or radio, or websites. And it is of no use as a vehicle for 'parenthetical' comments – asides – that you don't want to place in the body of your essay.

The author/page style

Varieties

The main (if not the only) version of this style is the MLA style, codified by the Modern Language Association in the USA.

Inserts in the text

In the text you place an insert giving the author(s) and the number of the page. For example: 'Jones (117) describes X as . . .' or 'X has been described (Jones 117) as . . .'. If you are referring to two different publications both authored by Jones, they are differentiated by including the title, which may be abbreviated.

Listing

At the end of your essay you attach a list of all the sources you have cited, in alphabetical order of authors' surnames. This list should be headed 'Works cited'.

Usefulness

The author/page style is most useful where all your sources are books or journal articles with one or more designated authors. If your source is an article in a bulky newspaper, citing the page is good practice since it will help the reader to track down the article. This style can also work satisfactorily even if no author is credited, because you can cite the title instead. It is less good with websites and, like the author/date style, is of no use as a vehicle for parenthetical comments that you don't want to place in the body of your essay.

The numbered-note style

Varieties

Numbered-note styles include the Chicago and Turabian styles well known in the USA. In Australia, the so-called Oxford style and Cambridge style are also of this kind. In the UK, you may find it referred to as the traditional footnote style or the endnote style, or – as by the British Standards Institution – the 'running notes' style.[3] It is commonly used in the arts and humanities, some social and political science fields, and law.

Inserts in the text

At every point where you wish to supply a reference or a comment of some kind, you insert a superscript, a raised number. You start with [1], then [2], and so on, through the essay. Even if you are referring to a source that you have already referred to, you give it a new number (so no superscript number appears twice). Variants of this style place the footnote number in round or square brackets. Footnote numbers should follow, not precede, full stops.

Listing

For every superscript, you write a note giving the reference and/or making your comment. These notes may be placed at the foot of the page on which the superscript appears, in which case they are footnotes, or at the end of the essay, in which case they are endnotes. The notes will be listed in numerical order to correspond with the superscripts. The list of endnotes can appro-priately be headed 'Notes and references'.

In addition to the list of notes and references, you may be asked by your teachers to provide a bibliography. Normally this would be a list of books and articles that you have used for 'background' reading: ask whether works listed in your notes should also be listed in your bibliography.

Usefulness

The great thing about the numbered-note style is that you can use it not only for references but for those parenthetical comments and asides that would interrupt the flow if you put them in the body of your text: a comment on the reliability of a source, or on some quirk that it exhibits; a reminder to the reader what certain abbreviations stand for; a signpost to another source where a different point of view can be found; and so on. It is also convenient to use when you are citing an original source which a secondary source led you to: you can simply cite the original and then say 'cited by' the secondary source.

The numbered-note style can be cumbersome if you've inserted all your superscripts and then decide you want to add or subtract a reference, because this entails renumbering all the subsequent references. One way of getting round this is by using your word processor's automatic footnote/endnote system. Another way is to type out each note within your text and enclose it within pairs of hash symbols: ## . . . ##. When you've finalized the text you can find these symbols one by one (using the 'Find' facility), remove each one from the text on to the clipboard and substitute the relevant superscript, and then copy them from the clipboard in batches of ten into your 'Notes and references' list.

The Vancouver-numeric style

Varieties

The Vancouver style emerged from a meeting of editors of general medical journals that was held in Vancouver, Canada, in 1978 to establish guidelines for the format of manuscripts submitted to their journals. The group agreed a set of guidelines which was first published in 1979 and defines the Vancouver style. The latest version, updated in October 2008, *Uniform Requirements for Manuscripts Submitted to Biomedical Journals: Writing and Editing for Biomedical Publication*,[4] is effectively the norm for biomedical journals. The numeric system described very briefly in BS 5605:1990[5] is very similar.

Inserts in the text

At every point where you wish to supply a reference to a source you have used, you insert a number in brackets (parentheses). (BS 5605:1990 offers the choice of using superscripts instead.) Similarly to numbered notes, you start with (1), then (2), and so on, through the essay. *But* when you refer to a source that you have previously referred to, you insert its *original* number (unlike the numbered-note style). So if you refer to source no. 3 seven times, say, the insert (3) will appear seven times in your text.

Listing

For every insert, you write a reference saying where the source can be found. Your list of references will go at the end of your essay, in numerical order to correspond with the inserts. The list can be headed 'References'.

Usefulness

Like the author/date style, the Vancouver-numeric style is most useful where all your sources are books or journal articles with one or more designated authors. The inserts are less distracting than authors, dates and page numbers. But if you have referred to different parts of the book in different places in your text it does not offer you an elegant method of citing the different page numbers in the book: it is therefore most effective where your sources are relatively compact, like journal articles or self-contained chapters in a book.

The Vancouver-numeric style is more economical than the numbered-note style in that only one reference is needed for each source (and so you will have no occasion to use the terms *ibid.*, *op. cit.* or *loc. cit.*: see Chapter 26). But it is less useful if you have to deal with 'messy' sources, and it is of no use as a vehicle for parenthetical comments.

Whichever referencing style you use for your essays, try to be 100 per cent accurate, complete and, above all, consistent. Academics have a keen eye for inconsistency and most of them thoroughly detest it. Many will mark you down for it. And pay attention to spelling authors' names correctly. A spell-checker won't help you with these, and wrongly spelled names, too, give a poor impression to the reader.

26

How to capture and list details of your sources

Citing sources will be easier to do if you make a habit of capturing – recording – their details at the time when you take notes from them. When you're photocopying pages from a book, save yourself some work by photocopying the title page too, because it will have some of the details you need (don't forget to add the year of publication to your photocopy).

I have one innovation to suggest: that you include among the details that you capture the ISBN (International Standard Book Number) for books and the ISSN (International Standard Serial Number) for journals. The former in particular is extremely useful. Search for it in a good academic library's online catalogue and you will immediately be shown all the other details of the book. You may find an ISBN in either a 13-digit or 10-digit form: both should work with online catalogues.

Printed academic sources

For a 'unitary' book (i.e. written as a whole, not a compilation of chapters by different authors), record the following:

■ the name(s) of the author(s)

■ the ISBN

■ the title and subtitle

■ the year of publication

■ the edition, if not the first

■ the publisher

■ the city or town where the publisher's main office is situated

■ the number(s) of the relevant pages.

For a chapter in a 'compilation' book:

- the name(s) of the author(s) of the chapter

- the ISBN

- the title of the chapter

- the title and subtitle of the book

- the name(s) of the editor(s) of the book

- the year of publication

- the publisher

- the city or town where the publisher's main office is situated

- the number(s) of the relevant pages.

For an article in a journal:

- the name(s) of the author(s)

- the journal's ISSN

- the title of the article

- the title of the journal and any standard abbreviation of the title

- the year of publication

- the number of the volume of the journal

- the part number of the journal and month (or season of the year) of publication

- the number(s) of the relevant pages.

Web pages

For an item on a web page, note down:

- the URL (uniform resource locator) of the page, otherwise known as its web address

- the date on which you accessed the page

- if the item is published in an electronic journal (e-journal), the ISSN of the journal, which should appear on its home page.

- if the item is a document – e.g. a Word file or a pdf file – also make a note of whatever information is provided about title, author, version and date of publication.

It is sensible to copy and paste the URL into a document to guard against errors in copying by hand, especially if the URL is one of those monster database-generated ones whose rhyme and reason are known only to the webmaster. Additionally, if that web page is reached by a series of clicks from a page with a short URL, make a note of that URL together with the directions (i.e. 'click on . . .') for reaching the relevant page. Remember that one of the purposes of referencing is to enable the reader to check your reasoning for himself or herself, and following directions to reach a web page may be easier and more straightforward than laboriously transcribing a monster URL.

Be sure, too, to store the web page electronically, and to print it out, so you have it to refer to if the page is subsequently altered or becomes unavailable. And watch out for line breaks (*never* insert a hyphen, as this will change the URL) and for underscores concealed by an underline.

Other sources

In addition to printed academic sources and web pages, there are numerous sources of other kinds: official publications, such as UK parliamentary papers and census reports; maps of various kinds; law reports; pamphlets and similar ephemera; and audio-visual material. For guidance on referencing these you need specialized advice, which your department or library should provide you with, or a more comprehensive treatment than is possible to provide here. Two useful sources are Colin Neville's *The Complete Guide to Referencing and Avoiding Plagiarism* (Open University Press, 2007, ISBN-13: 9780335220892), and the 2008 (or later) edition of *Cite Them Right: The Essential Referencing Guide* by Richard Pears and Graham Shields (Pear Tree Books, Newcastle-upon-Tyne, ISBN-13: 9780955121616).

Listing your references

If you are using the **author/date** (e.g. Harvard) or **author/page** style, you will need to have a reference list – i.e. a list of your sources – at the end of your essay. It should be arranged in alphabetical order of authors' (or first authors') surnames. For a single-author book, the layout of each item in the list will usually be as follows:

Author's surname | Author's initials or first name | Year of publication | Title (usually in italics but may be underlined) | Number of edition if not the first | Place of publication (followed by a colon) | Publisher

You may be required to provide, in addition to your list of sources, a bibliography: a list of texts that you have consulted. Some of these may also feature in your reference list, but there may be others that you have used for background reading but not drawn on for quotations or other specific material. The items in this bibliography should be laid out in the same way as those in your main reference list.

If you are using the **Vancouver-numeric style**, the items in your list of references will be arranged in the numerical order of your bracketed inserts. For a single-author book, the layout will be as follows:

Author's surname | Author's initials or first name (but these can go before the surname if preferred) | Title (usually in italics but may be underlined) | Number of edition if not the first | Place of publication (followed by a colon) | Publisher | Year of publication

As you can see, the main difference from the Harvard style is that the date of publication is placed at the end of the reference rather than directly after the author's name.

If you have to provide a bibliography, the items in it should be laid out in the same way as those in your main reference list.

If you are using the **numbered-note** style with endnotes (as opposed to footnotes, which appear on each page), your reference list will be arranged in the numerical order of your notes, as shown by the superscript number. This style does offer you some choice in laying out your references. For a single-author book, here are three slightly differing possibilities:

Note number | Author's surname | Author's initials or first name | Title | Number of edition if not the first | Place of publication (followed by a colon) | Publisher | Year of publication | Page number(s)

Note number | Author's initials or first name | Author's surname | Title | Number of edition if not the first | Place of publication (followed by a colon) | Publisher | Year of publication | Page number(s)

Note number | Author's initials or first name | Author's surname | Year of publication (in brackets) | Title | Number of edition if not the first | Page number(s) | Place of publication (followed by a colon) | Publisher

The items in your bibliography, if you are including one, should be laid out in the same fashion as those in your reference list, but without numbers and page numbers.

If you are using the numbered-note style, you may find yourself referring to the same source a number of times. There are conventions that you can use to save yourself copying out the reference afresh each time: the *'ibid.'*, *'op. cit.'* and *'loc. cit.'* conventions. *Ibid.* is an abbreviation of *ibidem*, a Latin word meaning 'in the same place'. *Op. cit.* is an abbreviation of *opere citato*, a Latin phrase meaning 'in the work cited'. *Loc. cit.* is an abbreviation of *loco citato*, Latin for 'in the place cited'. (As you can see, I'm adopting the convention here of putting words that are in a foreign language in italics.) You can use *ibid.* when a note refers to the same source as does the previous note, either the same page or a different one. You can use *op. cit.* to refer to a work previously cited in the same list. And you can use *loc. cit.* when you are referring to the same place in a work previously cited in the same list. For example:

18   P. Levin (1997) *Making Social Policy*, p. 30. Buckingham: Open University Press.
19   *Ibid.*, p. 65. [Same author and book as in previous note but different page]
20   *Ibid.* [Same author, same book and same page as in previous note]
21   J. G. March and H. A. Simon (1958) *Organizations*, pp. 140–1. New York: Wiley.
22   Levin, *op. cit.*, p. 222. [The work by Levin previously cited in this list, but a different page]
23   March and Simon, *loc. cit.* [The work by March and Simon previously cited in this list, and the same page]

If the use of Latin strikes you as too archaic for words, you can do something like this:

18   P. Levin (1997) *Making Social Policy*, p. 30. Buckingham: Open University Press.

19   Levin, note 18, p. 65. [Same author and book as in previous note but different page]

20   As note 19. [Same author, same book and same page as in previous note]

21   J. G. March and H. A. Simon (1958) *Organizations*, pp. 140–1. New York: Wiley.

22   Levin, note 18, p. 222. [The work by Levin previously cited in this list, but a different page]

23   As note 21. [The work by March and Simon previously cited in this list, and the same pages]

As ever, aim to be accurate, complete and consistent in listing your references.

Part 5

Plagiarism and collusion

27

The conscientious student's predicament

Plagiarism is a subject on which some academics these days are exceedingly twitchy. One hears of students submitting written work that in whole or in part appears to have been composed by other people, without citing its source. In some cases this is undoubtedly cheating (in the sense of acting with intention to deceive), as when large amounts of material have been 'lifted' – taken verbatim – from an unacknowledged source, or systematic efforts have been made to conceal the fact that other people's material has been used (e.g. attributing only some of the 'borrowed' material, changing the order of items in a list, making minor alterations in wording).

Understandably, cheating is taken particularly seriously when the mark for the work submitted will count towards the student's degree result, because if it is not detected he or she may be awarded a better result than they have earned. And this, of course, is seen as detrimental to the public standing of the institution's degrees, as well as grossly unfair to all the conscientious, law-abiding students who have worked hard for their results.

Universities have reacted to this situation in a predictable and often cack-handed manner, by producing their own definitions of 'plagiarism' and accompanying regulations, and issuing stern warnings couched in highly emotive language: plagiarism is 'cheating', 'stealing', 'dishonest', 'theft', 'a crime'. New students may have to sign plagiarism statements immediately on arrival saying they're aware of the seriousness of plagiarism and the penalties it incurs. So you turn up, stand in a queue to register, are told 'sign here', and given no time to read the small print. In effect, you are welcomed to the academic community with a message from your teachers saying: 'We regard you as potentially dishonest, a cheat and a thief, and we are watching you!'

(As it happens, 'theft' is defined in English law as follows: 'A person is guilty of theft if he dishonestly appropriates property belonging to another with the intention of permanently depriving the other of it . . .'.[1] Clearly someone who plagiarizes is *not* doing so with the intention of permanently depriving the original author of it. Nor could plagiarism fall under the criminal – as opposed to civil – law, as theft does.)

It all adds up to creating a threatening, intimidating atmosphere. An item in 2005 in *Online Scene*, published by Southampton University Students' Union, brings this out:

> Plagiarism! Every student attempting to write an essay has the word ringing in their ears. It provokes the same fear in everyone whether you're a first year or you're writing your dissertation.[2]

The stress that all this creates doesn't help you, of course. Lynn Errey cites an international postgraduate student:

> When I get nervous about writing up my thoughts in poor English even when I know the subject okay I can't think. So I use other people's words.[3]

Unsurprisingly, the regulations and warnings are often highly confusing. There tends to be a common core – you mustn't pass off other people's work as your own, which is fair enough – but they all give rise to more questions. If you unintentionally omit to cite a source, does that count as plagiarism? If you use two or three phrases that you dimly recollect from a lecture or some article you've read, without attributing them, does that make you guilty of plagiarism? How close to an unattributed original does paraphrasing have to be for it to be plagiarism? And what counts as 'common knowledge', so you don't need to reference it?

Different academics would give different answers to these questions. Many would regard unintentional failure to cite a source, or failure to attribute a dimly recollected phrase or two, or paraphrasing of an unattributed original into which some work has evidently been put, or an error of judgment as to what can be treated as common knowledge, as poor academic practice rather than outright cheating.

You may be further confused if your teachers insist that your work must be 'original'. This is another minefield! In fact, even a University of London MPhil thesis is not required to be original, so long as it is 'an ordered and critical exposition of existing knowledge and [provides] evidence that the field has been surveyed thoroughly'.[4] Logically, then, originality shouldn't be a necessary condition for gaining a bachelor's degree either. And I would respectfully suggest that the whole point of going to university and pursuing a degree course is that you *are* aided in your work, and that you *do* learn how to 'derive' your opinions and conclusions from the work of others, given that – as noted above – the focus of academic learning is the views of other people.

All in all, the current confusion surrounding plagiarism and originality creates a predicament for conscientious, hard-working, law-abiding students, and some have certainly been penalized for unwittingly breaking the university's rules on plagiarism, despite having no intention to cheat.

28

How academic learning forces you to plagiarize

One of the dictionary definitions of 'plagiarize' is 'to appropriate (ideas, passages, etc.) from (another work or author)'.[1] In this particular sense, plagiarism is actually integral to the Western system of propagating knowledge and ideas through higher education, because, to repeat Diana Laurillard's words, 'it is a peculiarity of academic learning that its focus is not the world itself but others' views of that world'.[2] The great majority of what you are required to learn is based on the documented views – the perceptions and thoughts – of others, not on your own experience. You read and listen, you copy out, you make your notes, you paraphrase (that's to say, you translate academic-speak into language you can understand), and you absorb, you digest, *other people's work*. Far from being 'cheating', appropriating from others is central to academic learning.

Getting a solid grounding in a subject must necessarily entail absorbing other people's views, internalizing them. Do this successfully and you won't know – you *can't* know – where your views begin and someone else's end. In much the same way as children are brought up by their parents and in the process take on unconsciously their attitudes, their ways of being and thinking and looking at the world, and of course their language, successful students undergo an analogous 'bringing-up' process in the course of becoming an historian or physicist or whatever, similarly picking up attitudes, ways of being and thinking, and – crucially – ideas and language: expressions, turns of phrase, ways of describing, explaining, arguing. Without the solid grounding created by such a process, you won't have a firm base on which to develop and build views of your own.

In Chapter 2, I suggested that academic learning proceeds in three repeating stages: (1) selecting and copying, as in making notes; (2) translating, as in paraphrasing and annotating; and (3) gaining understanding. In all of these stages you may risk being accused of plagiarism.

Selecting and copying

When you first take notes, the words are of course those of the author: they still 'belong' to that person. But the notes are *your* notes, and as you become familiar with them you appropriate them: you 'internalize' them, you incorporate them into your personal knowledge and understanding of the subject. So you are – *of necessity* – appropriating other people's material. And the more effectively that you do this, the more difficult it is to attribute sources.

Translating

Translating involves expressing the words that you read or hear into different words, so you produce an equivalent statement that, all being well, makes sense to you. That is to say, it involves you in *paraphrasing* the original statement. You can see from various definitions of plagiarism that paraphrasing carries the same dangers of plagiarizing as direct quoting does. Again, as with quotations, you are – of necessity – appropriating your paraphrasings as your own: you are 'internalizing' them, incorporating them into your personal understanding and conceptions of the subject matter. So translating too positively *forces* you to plagiarize (in the sense of appropriating the work of others), if only to yourself.

Gaining understanding

When you break through from selecting/copying and translating to gaining understanding of a topic, you are once more in danger of involuntary plagiarizing. When you're fluent in a subject, you're thinking and reasoning in its language unconsciously. To me, an appropriate analogy to this process is that of learning to dance. For some people, this involves first getting the moves into your head, then getting them into your feet, then getting them out of your head. At this point you're dancing without consciously thinking about it. For academics to demand of students who are fluent in a subject that they cite in a piece of written work every source that they've drawn on is like insisting that they learn to dance with their shoes tied together.

It's not only students who encounter this difficulty. You may be interested to see a 43-page report prepared in May 2001 for the Joint Information Systems Committee: *Plagiarism: A Good Practice Guide.* (Don't be confused by its title: this is not a guide to making a good job of plagiarizing.) Its authors, Jude Carroll and Jon Appleton, acknowledge that their suggestions and recommendations arise from a range of sources, not all of which they have cited:

> Some . . . are gleaned from the experience of colleagues or more experienced practitioners, from conversations with a wide range of people at conferences, and from consultations with student representatives . . . Where appropriate, sources and research findings are cited but it has not always been possible to unearth the exact origin of ideas or to use publicly available sources.[3]

The fact that experts in detecting plagiarism don't always find it possible to unearth the exact origin of ideas they have used, sits oddly with the frequently encountered injunction to students that *they* must do so. And I think it corroborates my suggestion that taking in other people's ideas is something that can happen at a subconscious level, and that the nature of academic learning, where you are required to absorb the work of others, is such that it positively *forces* you to begin by plagiarizing, if only to yourself.

Incidentally, there is no copyright in ideas. The UK Intellectual Property Office demolishes this notion succinctly and comprehensively. 'Copyright doesn't protect ideas. The work must be fixed (e.g. written or recorded)' in order to be protected.[4] Cite your sources where you can, but you should be congratulated, not penalized, for latching on to ideas that are floating around in the academic stratosphere and have been cut adrift from whatever 'exact origins' they may have had.

If plagiarism is so deeply engrained in the academic culture, how can you avoid laying yourself open to being accused of it? In the next chapter I offer some suggestions as to what you can do.

29

Avoiding accusations of plagiarism

The best way of avoiding accusations of plagiarism is to develop good academic practice. In a sense, the whole of this book has been about developing good academic practice. Here are some final points.

Question what you read

Get into the habit of questioning everything that you read. Ask yourself: 'Where does the writer get this from? How does he or she know? What assumptions or value judgments are being made here? How can I test that theory or model?' Check your answers with your teacher, at least while you're still gaining your confidence. This is a very good way of getting into the mindset of writers and developing the skill of reading critically.

There is an important point here for master's students who have done their first degree at a different university, especially one outside the UK. You may previously have been in an educational system where you were expected to be able to quote authorities and textbooks, and were rewarded for doing no more than this. At your present university it may not be the same. You are likely to find that you are expected to *use* quotations to answer the question set for you. In other words, you have to 'digest' the quotations you want to use – not merely reproduce them – and show in your essay that you have understood their relevance to the topic.

Collusion: Take care when working with other students!

You may find that you are warned not only against committing plagiarism but also against committing 'collusion', conspiring with one or more other students to improve your marks by working together. Of course, students have always worked together – these may be among your most memorable and valuable learning experiences – and today we have the bizarre situation that many UK universities are, on the one hand, actually encouraging students to develop their teamwork skills, yet on the other hand they are warning them against collusion.

How should you respond to these mixed messages? I would certainly encourage you to work with other students: you will learn from them as well as from your teachers, and you will usually be able to express ideas and ask questions without feeling that you are being judged, which may not be the case in 'official' tutorials, classes and seminars. And you may find essays written by other students easier to learn from than texts written by academics, because they are written by people who are at a similar stage of the learning process to yourself. Indeed, you may find them mercifully free from the academic-speak and pontificating to which many academics are sadly prone. But do stop short of drafting essays or parts of essays together. The final selection of words must emerge from your own mind: it must be your own. Otherwise the sniffers-out of plagiarism will be on your tracks.

And beware the temptation to be altruistic and show your work to somebody else who persuades you that they need help. If the other person copies some of your work, both you and the other person will be penalized if the copying is detected. And if the authorities are unable to say who is copying whom, you won't even gain credit for being the original author.

Claim copyright for your own work

It is not unknown for academics to get ideas from their students and pass them off as their own. If an essay is genuinely your own work, and if you have properly acknowledged material drawn from other sources, the copyright in what you have written belongs to you: morally, legally and automatically. Indeed, if you have had to sign some kind of declaration that it is your own work, it follows that copyright belongs to you. There is no official registration for copyright,[1] but you can do what many authors do: add © Your Name 2009 (or whatever the year is) at the foot of the title page or at the end of the document. (In Micrososft Word, for © type Ctrl+Alt+C.)

Resist off-the-shelf offerings

If you are one of a large cohort of students taking a course, it may sometimes feel as though having to supply essays at regular intervals is exactly like having to satisfy a dog by providing it with regular meals. The temptation is to do the equivalent of going to the supermarket, purchasing a tin of dog food, opening it and spooning it into a bowl. Beware! Academics want home-prepared food, and they are going to judge you on it, which is why they are so antagonistic to your passing off shop-bought food as home-made. Even if you are using bought-in, ready-to-use ingredients, you must add something of your own – an extra ingredient or two, for example, or a variation on the method of preparation, cooking or presentation. Do your own little research project: try to work out what it is that will give your offerings 'teacher appeal'. But note that teachers, like dogs, are not all alike: subtle variations may be necessary to appeal to different academic tastes.

To plagiarize and successfully conceal the fact is hard work. You may as well devote that effort to doing the job properly. Don't be tempted, even if you are up against a deadline, to buy an essay from an outfit advertising on the internet and submit it as your own work. This really is asking for trouble. Doing this raises no subtle questions of what is meant by plagiarism: it is an absolutely clear-cut case of cheating. The existence of highly developed plagiarism-detection software today makes it almost certain that you will be found out. You will be severely penalized – possibly being refused a degree or expelled from the institution – and subjected to a great deal of public humiliation, involving being branded as dishonest and a cheat. So I definitely do not recommend this course of action. Even if you submit a handwritten essay, it is almost impossible to avoid giving clues if you have used someone else's material word-for-word or in a close paraphrasing. Most academics love detective work, especially if they can feel righteous about it, and you are challenging them in their specialist field. Don't even try!

I would just add that in my experience students who actively try to master the language of their subjects, who question what they read, who read more than one book on a topic and check out original sources, and who actively seek feedback from their teachers and discuss their subjects with other students, tend to be the ones who get good results. Try to be one of them, and passing off other people's work as your own is the last thing you'll need to do in order to get good marks.

30

The politics of plagiarism

Check out your institution's rules and regulations

It will pay you to become familiar with your institution's rule book, code of practice, or whatever, on the subject of plagiarism. This will help you to keep out of trouble, and to keep a level head if there are rumours flying around about what does and does not count as plagiarism. And if you get on the wrong side of any of your teachers, knowing the rules and conforming to them will help you to avoid giving someone an excuse to accuse you of breaking them.

Notice how the rules are constituted. The more lengthy and detailed they are, and the more attention they give to spelling out offences rather than offering help, the more likely it is that those who drew them up are afflicted by paranoia on the subject. There may not be much that you can do about that, but you should at least be aware of it.

Keep an eye open too for inconsistencies in the rules. They provide evidence of the confusion that exists among academics. A policy riddled with inconsistencies and rooted in confusion is always open to challenge. Look out, too, for words and phrases that require those who enforce rules to make judgments in interpreting them: 'substantial', 'extensive use', etc. Such judgments too may well be open to challenge.

Finally, if you are expected to cite your sources in a particular style – it will usually be the Harvard style or the numbered-note style – make sure you know what you're doing. If you're given a style guide, follow it. If you aren't supplied with one, ask where you can get one.

Check out your institution's practices

Rules and regulations are one thing; how they are enforced in practice may be quite another. Someone in your students' union should have the job of keeping track of hearings into cases of alleged plagiarism, and reading reports on cases, paying particular attention to the evidence and criteria on which decisions were taken. He or she should be able to tell whether the institution is primarily concerned to prevent cheating or to enforce every minute detail of its plagiarism code and inflict the full force of the disciplinary machinery even on small-scale, inadvertent transgressions.

Note how much discretion the academics have. It may be a matter for their judgment (a) whether the evidence supports the allegation that plagiarism has taken place; (b) if it does, whether it is a mild or severe offence; (c) whether there are extenuating circumstances; and (d) what the penalty should be. Different people may make different judgments (academics disagree with one another) and the membership of committees changes from year to year. Whether a student appears at a hearing or not, and is represented or not, may also influence the judgments that are made. However, a student accused of plagiarism is entitled to expect that his or her treatment will be consistent with previous cases, and if your institution shows what appears to be an undue concern with 'petty' plagiarism it will be worth examining the records of past cases to see whether they have been treated consistently: have similar cases incurred similar penalties?

It would also be worth inspecting cases to see whether students have been penalized for what is really poor academic practice rather than plagiarism. The line between these may well be blurred, in which case where it is drawn in a particular case may well be open to challenge.

Finally, you may also be able to challenge decisions if the regulations are imprecise, or it has not been made clear to you how they would apply in common situations: if, for example, you have not been told whether, if you have an idea that you think is your very own, you will be penalized or not if it turns out later that it's in someone's book. Or if you have not been told how to judge whether something can be taken as common knowledge, and therefore does not need to be referenced.

Notes and references

The strange world of the university

1. Diana Laurillard, *Rethinking University Education* (Routledge, 1993), ch. 1 and p. 50.
2. White Paper, *The Future of Higher Education*, Cm 5735 (The Stationery Office, 2003), para. 1.18.
3. The 2008 National Student Survey of nearly 220,000 final-year students found that around 40 per cent of students in England were dissatisfied with the feedback they had received on their work. 'Buckingham tops national student survey', *The Guardian*, 11 September 2008. Available online at http://www.guardian.co.uk/education/2008/sep/11/student.survey (accessed 1 March 2009).

1 'I'm a slow reader'

1. Reported in *The Times Higher Education Supplement*, Textbook Guide, 28 May 2004, p. II.

3 Making notes and translating 'academic-speak'

1. Peter J. Larkham, Exploring and dealing with plagiarism: traditional approaches. Available online at http://www.jiscpas.ac.uk/images/bin/larkham_plagiarism_text.pdf (accessed 1 March 2009).

7 Exploratory reading (2): How to use the World Wide Web

1. Websearch workshop 'Search Engines'. Available online at: http://www.websearchworkshop.co.uk/search-engines.php (accessed 1 March 2009).
2. http://www.aber.ac.uk/media/Students/hrb9701.html (accessed 1 March 2009).

3. http://www.aber.ac.uk/media/Students/ (accessed 1 March 2009).
4. Can one be the second person to coin a term?
5. http://en.wikipedia.org/wiki/Moral_panic (accessed 1 March 2009).
6. http://en.wikipedia.org/wiki/Jock_Young (accessed 1 March 2009).
7. The full title of this paper is 'The role of the police as amplifiers of deviance, negotiators of reality and translators of fantasy'.
8. http://bjc.oxfordjournals.org/cgi/content/full/azn074. The full title of this paper is 'Moral panic: its origins in resistance, ressentiment and the translation of fantasy into reality'. (Abstract accessed 1 March 2009.)

10 How to work with secondary sources

1. J. Underwood and A. Szabo, *Plagiarism: Is this a Problem in Tertiary Education* (JISCPAS, undated but 2003 or later), p. 2. Available online at www.jiscpas.ac.uk/images/bin/underwoodtertiary.pdf (accessed 1 March 2009).
2. As above.
3. J. Carroll, *Institutional Issues in Deterring, Detecting and Dealing with Student Plagiarism* (JISC, August 2004), p. 1. Available online at www.jisc.ac.uk/uploaded_documents/plagFinal.pdf (accessed 1 March 2009).
4. As above, p. 4.
5. R. Graham and M. Hart, 'Plagiarism is a complex issue, but – universities must articulate a moral vision and live up to it!' Paper delivered at the 4th European Conference on Research Methodology for Business and Management Studies (ECRM, 2005), Université Paris-Dauphine 21–22 April 2005, para. 3.1. Available online at www.business-kac.co.uk/plag_com2.doc (accessed 1 March 2009).
6. As above, para. 9.5.

15 How your essay will be marked (1): 'Tick-box' marking

1. University of Exeter, *Supplementary Assessment Matters, Undergraduate Generic Mark Scheme*. Available online at http://admin.exeter.ac.uk/academic/tls/tqa/Part%208/8Padvice1.pdf (accessed 3 July 2009). This mark scheme is remarkable for devoting 102 words to describing three categories of First class mark, nearly as many as the total for all other classes (including 'fail') put together (111). The 2:2 class gets only 15 words.

2. The Kent page is available online at http://www.kent.ac.uk/uelt/academic-practice/apt-dev-prog/podcasts/rust/essay-criteria.pdf. The Leeds page, which has a word missing, is available online at http://www.leeds.ac.uk/sddu/lt/teachtalk/docs/white%20sheet.pdf (both accessed 1 March 2009).

3. http://www.kent.ac.uk/uelt/academic-practice/apt-dev-prog/podcasts/rust/ (accessed 1 March 2009).

16   How your essay will be marked (2): Impressionistic marking

1. *Firsts among Equals?*, broadcast on BBC2, 5 November 1996.

20   How to use quotations

1. Metaphor: a figure of speech in which a word or phrase is applied to an object or action that it does not literally denote, e.g. 'an entrenched tradition'. Simile: a figure of speech that expresses the resemblance of one thing to another of a different category, e.g. 'He turned as red as a beetroot'.

23   Writer's block and how to overcome it

1. This example of the use of a 'question string' is taken from my book *Sail through Exams!* (another Student-Friendly Guide published by Open University Press, 2004).

25   Which style to choose?

1. APA American Psychological Association; ASA/ASR American Sociological Association/*American Sociological Review*; CBE Council of Biology Editors; AIP American Institute of Physics.

2. R. M. Ritter, *The Oxford Guide to Style* (Oxford University Press, 2002), p. 505.

3. British Standards Institution, BS 5605:1990 *Recommendations for Citing and Referencing Published Material* (BSI, 1990).

4. International Committee of Medical Journal Editors, *Uniform Requirements for Manuscripts Submitted to Biomedical Journals: Writing and Editing for Biomedical Publication*, updated October 2008. Available online at http://www.icmje.org/ (accessed 1 March 2009).

5. British Standards Institution, as note 3.

27 The conscientious student's predicament

1. Theft Act 1968, S.1(1). This section available online at http://www.legislation.gov.uk/RevisedStatutes/Acts/ukpga/1968/cukpga_19680060_en_1 (accessed 2 June 2009).
2. 'Students cheating to the top', *Online Scene* (Southampton University Students Union, 29 December 2005. Available online at http://www.wessexscene.co.uk/news/1393 (accessed 14 May 2009).
3. L. Errey, 'Plagiarism: Something fishy? . . . Or just a fish out of water?', *Teaching Forum*, vol. 50 (Autumn 2002), p. 18. Available online at http://www.brookes.ac.uk/virtual/NewTF/50/T50errey.pdf (accessed 1 March 2009).
4. These regulations are available online at http://www.london.ac.uk/fileadmin/documents/students/postgraduate/MPhil.PhD_regs_from_Sept_2008.pdf (accessed 1 March 2009).

28 How academic learning forces you to plagiarize

1. *Collins English Dictionary* (Collins Dictionary of the English Language, 1979).
2. Diana Laurillard, *Rethinking University Education* (Routledge, 1993), Ch. 1 and p. 50.
3. J. Carroll and J. Appleton, *Plagiarism: A Good Practice Guide* (JISC, May 2001), p. 8. Available online at http://www.jisc.ac.uk/uploaded_documents/brookes.pdf (accessed 1 March 2009).
4. Intellectual Property Office, *Fast Facts*. Available online at http://www.ipo.gov.uk/types/copy.htm (accessed 1 March 2009). The IPO is the official government body responsible for granting intellectual property rights in the UK.

29 Avoiding accusations of plagiarism

1. Intellectual Property Office, *Fast Facts*. Available online at http://www.ipo.gov.uk/types/copy.htm (accessed 1 March 2009).

Books on speed reading

All of these books are published in paperback and were in print in early 2009.

Tony Buzan, *The Speed Reading Book* (revised edition, BBC Active, 2006)

Tina Konstant, *Teach Yourself Speed Reading* (Hodder Headline, 2003)

Paul R. Scheele, *PhotoReading* (4th edition, Learning Strategies Corporation, 2007)

Gordon R. Wainwright, *How to Read Faster, Recall More* (3rd edition, How To Books, 2006)

Acknowledgments

Many people have contributed, in many different ways, to this book. I owe a personal thank you to:

The many students who over the years have talked to me about their experiences of essay writing in higher education, and especially those who have given me feedback on the first edition of this book. It has been a great privilege to listen to them and work with them.

My former colleagues in the LSE Teaching and Learning Centre – especially Liz Barnett (Director), Jean Jameson and Sue Haines – who provided me with a congenial and supportive work environment.

Kate Slay, manager of the LSE Students' Union shop, who displayed and sold hundreds of copies of the self-published forerunner of this book.

Shona Mullen, Melanie Havelock and their colleagues at the Open University Press, whose encouragement, understanding and skill I have every reason to appreciate.

Kate Pool and her colleagues of the Society of Authors, for practical and moral support.

John Levin for his informed comments on early drafts of this book, for the benefit of lessons he learned in the UK higher education system, for his invaluable help with IT and support in the ongoing battle with Microsoft products, and especially for the pleasure of his company.

Rachel Adriano, who recently re-entered into the education system after a very long interval, and whose support for this project I value enormously.

Alice Pizer, for her belief in the importance of my work and writing.

Audrey Cleave, for demonstrating how a youthful, open mind can last and last.

Kevin Fitzgerald and Joe Geraghty, who both know about reinventing themselves: inspirations both.

Clare, Amy and Anne for their affection and encouragement and for road testing some of the ideas in this book.

Gill, my wife, for her loving care and support, for the memorable times we have together, and for her tolerance (mostly) of a quirky, untidy and often preoccupied author.

EXCELLENT DISSERTATIONS!

Peter Levin

"Such well thought through and clearly explained support tools are a breath of fresh air!"

BSc Social Policy student

Producing a dissertation is a major requirement of an increasing number of courses. The dissertation is likely to be the largest single piece of work you will be asked to produce. *Excellent dissertations!* guides you through the whole process: planning your dissertation project, managing it, and writing it up. This book offers friendly and practical advice. It addresses all the questions students ask, including:

- How do I choose a topic?
- How should I manage my time?
- How can I make best use of my supervisor?
- How many chapters should my dissertation have?
- Which is the best referencing system to use?

Excellent dissertations! is a must for every student with a dissertation to do. It is a lively, concise, and to-the-point guide, which will steer you through the entire process.

Contents: *List of Tables – List of Boxes – Producing a dissertation. READ THIS FIRST! – Introduction – Part One: Preliminaries – Formal requirements and arrangements – Pleasing the examiners – You and your supervisor – Part Two: Getting started – The 'twin-track': Your project and your dissertation – Project and dissertation: Exploring the literature – Project: Making a shortlist of possible subjects – Project: Selecting your preferred subject – Project: Methodology – Project: Materials – Project and dissertation: Time management and planning – Part Three: The 'middle period' – Keeping everything under control – Project: Being your own manager – Dissertation: Creating your literature review – Dissertation: Developing your outline – Part Four: The 'end-game' – The challenge to complete – Project: Concluding your work – Dissertation: Producing your first draft and finalizing your outline – Dissertation: Improving your draft – Dissertation: Conforming to good academic practice – Dissertation: Final editing – Notes and references – Acknowledgments.*

2005 136pp
978-0-335-21822-6 (Paperback)

SAIL THROUGH EXAMS!

Peter Levin

"A good read. The clear explanations of how to prepare for exams and ways to choose and answer questions are practical and useful."
BA Geography student

"Relevant for exams and how I should approach my studies. It was easy to synthesize the information given – and comforting! My problems don't seem unique to me any more."
MSc Management student

This lively, concise and to-the-point guide offers hints and practical suggestions to help you develop good exam-preparation skills and build your confidence, so that you can get results that do justice to the work you've put in.

■ How to use past exam papers
■ How to decode difficult-to-understand exam questions
■ How to structure top-quality answers
■ How to revise effectively
■ How to get in the right frame of mind for exams
■ How to do your best on the day

A must for every student preparing for traditional exams!

Contents: *List of Checklists – List of Boxes – The strange world of university examinations. READ THIS FIRST! – Introduction – Part One: Using past exam papers – Get hold of past exam papers – What to look for in past exam papers – Unfair questions – The guessing game: What topics will come up this year? – Part Two: Formulating model answers – Interpreting the question – Methodology – Materials – Drawing up a plan – An alternative approach: the 'question string' – Choose your introduction – Argument or chain of reasoning? – Writing exam answers: some more suggestions – Questions for examiners – Part Three: In the run-up to exams – Revising effectively – Memorizing – Make best use of your time – Getting in the right frame of mind for exams – Part Four: On the day of the exam – Be organized – Further Reading – Acknowledgments.*

2004 112pp
978-0-335-21576-8 (Paperback)

CONQUER STUDY STRESS!

Peter Levin

Are you finding student life stressful? Does the pressure get you down sometimes? Do other people seem to be coping much better than you? Could you use some friendly advice?

This book will help you by showing how to beat twenty of the most common causes of student stress. It describes the symptom, gives a diagnosis and offers tried and tested remedies. It covers such features of student life as:

- The culture shock facing new students
- Reading and note-taking and monster reading lists
- Writing under pressure
- Finding a dissertation subject and reviewing the literature
- The lack of constructive feedback
- The plagiarism police
- Pressure on your time
- Counselling services
- Exams

Contents: *Preface – Stressed out by induction – Intimidated by monster reading lists – Reading takes forever – On a different planet from your teachers – Knee-deep in notes – Suffering from writer's block – Mystified by essay topics – Demoralized by 'negative feedback' – Let down by poor spelling – Stumped for a dissertation subject – Bored with reviewing the literature – Feeling your opinion is worthless – Spooked by the plagiarism police – Getting good marks for coursework, poor marks in exams – Terrified by the prospect of exams – In a project group sabotaged by a 'free-rider' – Hopeless at time management – Tongue-tied in seminars – Unsure about the quality of counselling – Feeling like dropping out – Notes and references.*

2007 136pp
978-0-335-22865-2 (Paperback)